Sacred Intelligence

The Essence of Sacred, Selfish, and Shared Relationships

by

Terrlyn L. Curry Avery, PhD, MDiv

Sacred Intelligence, Published February, 2015

Editorial and Proofreading Services: Kellyann Zuzulo, Karen Grennan

Interior Layout and Cover Design: Howard Johnson, Howard Communigrafix, Inc.

Photo Credits: Cover: Depositphotos, Purple Sunset, 5392699

 **SDP Publishing**

Published by SDP Publishing, an imprint of SDP Publishing Solutions, LLC.

For more information about this book contact Lisa Akoury-Ross by email at lross@SDPPublishing.com.

SDP Publishing
Permissions Department
PO Box 26, East Bridgewater, MA 02333
or email your request to info@SDPPublishing.com.

ISBN-13 (print): 978-0-9905596-7-2
ISBN-13 (ebook): 978-0-9905596-8-9

Library of Congress Control Number: 2014959265

Printed in the United States of America

Here's what professionals are saying about "Sacred Intelligence"

"When someone expresses in writing what you need to hear to shift your life, all you can do is reply with gratitude. I thought my racing through life meant I was being ambitious. Through *Sacred Intelligence*, I now realize that racing is not living and in order to really *live* life, I need to alter my relationship with my*self*. Self? Yeah, trust me, read this book and you will know exactly what I mean. I am excited for all who will explore the magic of these words!"

— **Erin Saxton,** *Emmy Nominated TV Producer*

"Terrlyn L. Curry Avery has struck a nerve in her book *Scared Intelligence*. At a time when digital followers on social network sites are often mistaken for real flesh-and-blood relationships, she shows us how the relational landscape can be a virtual landmine of abuse that produces unhealthy action and attitudes.

There aren't a lot of resources to help someone develop positive relationships and heal from toxic ones. Dr. Curry Avery provides a methodology of stories, Scripture, reflections, powerful questions and exercises to assist the reader in developing their own sacred intelligence.

This is a great book to remind some and teach others that relationships make a difference in our lives. Strong positive ones can help us enjoy life, lengthen life, cut the risk of debilitating depression and even boost our immune systems. Who knew! Now, let's do the work!"

— **Bishop Vashti Murphy Mckenzie,** The 117th Elected and Consecrated Bishop of the African Methodist Episcopal (AME) Church, Author of "Journey to the Well"

"This beautiful book is a testament to Dr. Curry Avery's own sacred intelligence. Through stories and insightful reflections, she gently takes us on a path to a richer, and more fulfilling life of relationship with the sacred, ourselves, and others. The book is grounded not only in her experience as a psychologist and as an ordained Presbyterian minister, but also in her stance towards the sacred, her family, and all humankind, including those of all faiths and of no faith at all. The book reflects Dr. Curry Avery's deep understanding of the present moment in our noisy, overextended, and over-stimulated lives. With exercises and her own inspirational poetry, her book guides us to stillness, where we might find the strength to heal our lives and our relationships."

— **Adele Reinhartz,** *PhD, FRSC, Professor and Director of Graduate Programs Department of Classics and Religious Studies, University of Ottawa*

"Dr. Curry Avery calls us all into meditative spaces to reflect on the significant and unending relationships of humanity. This engaging and insightful work explores the realities of relationships in refreshing and dynamic ways. It encourages us to embrace the joys of being created 'in the image of God.'"

—**Rev. Dr. Yvonne Collie-Pendleton,** *Presbyterian Church (USA)*

"*Sacred Intelligence* is an honest and meaningful reflection on how living with integrity can help fortify our emotional "houses". By combining spiritual texts, psychological theory, anecdotes from her personal experiences, and thoughtful questions, Dr. Curry Avery invites the reader on a journey toward continual transformation. Those willing to do the work will be richly rewarded."

—**Dr. Jacqueline Hernandez,** *Licensed Clinical and School Psychologist*

"*Sacred Intelligence* presents a beautiful marriage of faith and cognitive-behavioral principles that therapists and those seeking help will find inspiring and enlightening.

Dr. Curry Avery provides many tools for meaningful self-reflection through pertinent stories and tips for practical activities that will enhance one's life and relationships with others. I highly recommend it to anyone looking to move forward in their life."

—**Rhonda Lewis Williams,** *Ph.D., Licensed Psychologist*

"Dr. Curry Avery's concept of "selfish intimacy" was foreign to me … everything and everyone else came first in my life. Now I know this powerful term is paramount in seeking God's face. Embracing it has helped me become an open vessel that God can use."

—**Jolynn R. Kendrick,** *MSW, Attorney's Assistant*

"*Sacred Intelligence* spoke to me and reminded me to be quiet and listen to the small voice of God. Doing so has helped me to grow in every area of my life, especially how I interact with others whether on a personal or professional level!"

—**Francine J. Vaughan,** *Business Owner*

Contents

To my parents, Elcue and Elmira Curry, who taught me the profound love of the Sacred, the importance of loving myself, and the value of sharing love with others.

To my husband, Dion, and children, Ruby and Teala: May the endowed love of the Sacred propel you to fulfill your highest calling and share your gifts with others.

In Memory
Vanessa A. Curry

ACKNOWLEDGMENTS

A book about sacred intelligence and the relationships that lead to such an awareness could not have been written without the invaluable relationships that influenced my life and helped to shape this book. Thank you to my editor, Kellyann Zuzulo, for your valuable comments, questions, insights, and guidance. To Lisa Akoury-Ross, my publisher: You made my experience enjoyable. I am grateful for your honesty and guidance throughout this process.

Thank you, Dr. John Gravely, who is now deceased, and the Rev. Carlton Elliott Smith for written contributions and invaluable support. Carlton, your listening ear and sustained friendship are forever engraved upon my heart.

Thank you, Susan Bainbridge, Donald Bliss, Loretta Curry, and Regina Curry for your editorial assistance through various phases of this book, as well as the innumerable other ways you helped me. Thank you, Christine Fortune and Lesley Ingves for your sharp attention to detail and "word-smith" genius.

I am indebted to the clients and participants of my retreats, who have taught me a great deal and allowed me the opportunity to help them strengthen their relationships. Thank you to friends, families, and supporters for your continued encouragement. In many ways, this book would not have been possible without the sustained sacrifices of my sister, Devarieste Curry, who forced me to correct letters written to her as a child, spent long hours nurturing my writing, demanded that I strive for excellence, and demonstrated unconditional love every step of the way.

I am immensely grateful to the thoughtfulness and psychological insights of Dr. Rosell Jenkins. You have been a great support, strong advocate, tough critic, and wonderful friend throughout the evolution of my career journey.

I want to express my sincerest gratitude to my ancestors and the Waterford, Mississippi, community; in particular, Mrs. Mattie Wilson and Mr. Melvin Ford for "paving the way" for me indirectly and directly. I will forever be grateful for my loving parents, Elcue and Elmira Curry, and my siblings, whose faith in God, indescribable love, strong belief in me, and numerous prayers help to shape my sacred, selfish, and shared relationships. I am who I am because of you. Dion, Ruby, and Teala, thank you for your sacrifices as you have traveled this road with me. The giving of your time and energy and often setting aside your own desires have not gone unnoticed as I have honored my calling. I love each of you!

I thank God, my Sacred source, who is ever-present and guides my every footstep!

Terrlyn's Story

My father was a playful and prayerful, embracing and expressive, witty and wise, and insightful and intelligent man. He was an imperfect, loving man who had a wonderful way of knowing—knowing about God,[1] knowing about himself, and knowing about other people, especially his children. He could read us like a book, recognizing when something was amiss with us even before we knew. He knew us better than we knew ourselves. I believe it was this intimate knowledge of each of his children that led him, two years prior to his death, to share with me his desire for me to do his eulogy.

I was honored, shocked, and amazed. I am the youngest of my parents' ten children. *Why me? What was he thinking?* What would I say? These questions were all part of my initial reaction to my father's decision to choose me. In my conversations with him about his choice, I realized that he had chosen me because he had been an integral part of my faith journey and preparation to become a minister. He knew that I would tout his good qualities but would not hesitate to mention his imperfections. Most importantly, he chose me because he knew he would prepare his eulogy for me and that I would be in tune with him and the Sacred to receive and share this gift.

In October of 2010, I was preparing a women's retreat on building and maintaining healthy relationships. I wanted to use the analogy of building a house, so I did what most people do and searched the Internet for help. After a few frustrating searches, I realized that I was going to the wrong source. I simply needed to ask my father, who had been a brick mason all of his life. So I called him just as I often did to discuss my sermons or get his opinion on some other matter.

After his usual greeting of "Hi Ms. Avery, how are you doing?" I explained to him the goal of my retreat.

"Well, baby," he said. "The first thing you need is a firm foundation. Your foundation has to be strong enough to withstand the storm." I knew that, for my father, this foundation was God.

As he began describing how to build a house, I must admit that I thought he did not understand what I was asking and I almost interrupted. The voice of the Sacred said, "Wait, just listen."

He continued. "Building a house requires good walls. Walls that must be selected from the best pieces of wood. The walls are built on the foundation and are supported by that foundation. It is within these walls that you learn to love and care for yourself."

My father, in his 85-year-old wisdom, then described the importance of the roof. "If the roof doesn't protect your walls, they could fall down. What this means is that you have to be careful who you hang around. Because the people you hang around can subtly punch holes in your protective covering and expose your walls to the elements. And these elements can determine where you are going in life. If your walls become too damaged, you might not have the resources to repair them."

I listened in amazement to this man who only had an eighth-grade education describe the psychology of building our emotional houses. He ended the conversation by expressing the need for strong reinforcers for the house. "You see, baby, your reinforcers are things that are powerful and that will strengthen you. You have to look at the instructions you have received. Keep studying and applying them . . . just like you went to school to study the Bible. If you don't apply what you learned and seek to gain more knowledge, your education will mean nothing. You'll forget what you learned and revert back to your old ways."

Wow! My listening paid off. In this brief conversation, my father put into words what he and my mother had taught us throughout our lives. I had all the information I needed for my retreat and so much more. I called my second oldest sibling and said to her, "Daddy just gave me his eulogy."

I knew it would not be long before his death. Throughout his remaining painful days, I witnessed my father's firm foundation in God sustain him. I saw him continue to build walls of protection around his family as he provided a spiritual covering for us as we faced his transition. He often prayed and sang songs of God's mercy and grace, not only to remind him that he was not alone, but to remind us of the Sacred's constant presence with us in all circumstances. I learned as much about my father from his dying as I did from his life.

In July 2011, my father died, and I delivered his eulogy four days prior to my ordination as a minister. I had accomplished the task he set before me and realized what he had done for me. In selecting me, he had authenticated my title as a minister for members of my family. Even more profoundly, he had left a legacy for generations to come. We build the best houses by establishing a firm foundation (the Sacred), selecting the best walls (Selfish), keeping them covered (Shared), and reinforcing them with powerful resources.

INTRODUCTION

You shall love the Lord your God with all your heart, and with all your soul, and with all your strength, and with all your mind; and your neighbor as yourself. —**Luke 10:27**[2]

Relationships are crucial to how we experience life. If we tend to have strong, happy, and positive relationships with others, we usually experience life in a more optimistic and uplifting way. If we have weak, unhappy, and negative relationships with others, we tend to be more pessimistic and disillusioned with life. These experiences not only help us to form our opinions of others but our opinions of ourselves, as well. We learn to love ourselves and feel confident in who we are, or we learn to dislike ourselves and second guess our worth, judgment, and skills.

The types of relationships we have with others are generally the result of past experiences that have shaped our way of thinking. For example, we might have had a negative interaction with a particular person or individuals from a particular group. As a result, we approach this person or persons in a manner that continues to perpetuate our thoughts (good or bad) about the experience. Both our experiences and opinions of ourselves have a profound impact on how we choose to relate to others. For instance, if we have a healthy and balanced opinion of ourselves, we are likely to treat others with respect and kindness. An unhealthy opinion, however, can result in hostility and disrespect toward others and feelings of anger, hatred, disappointment, and rejection of ourselves.

Regardless of the relationships we have with others (shared) or ourselves (selfish), both can be greatly enhanced by the relationship that we have with the Sacred. Understanding, knowing, and accepting that there is a greater power directing our paths and a greater power that loves us unconditionally, help us to share that love and ultimately create better relationships with others and ourselves. In other words, our relationships are interdependent; each impacts the other. The essence of our sacred, selfish, and shared relationships is our *Sacred Intelligence*. I define *Sacred Intelligence* as the ability to tap into our internal sacred source to make intelligent choices that will honor the Sacred and help us manifest our greatness, while simultaneously embracing the sacredness and humanity of others. If we were to visualize *Sacred Intelligence*, it might look like the Venn diagram below. The three overlapping circles represent each relationship with *Sacred Intelligence* as the core of the circles.

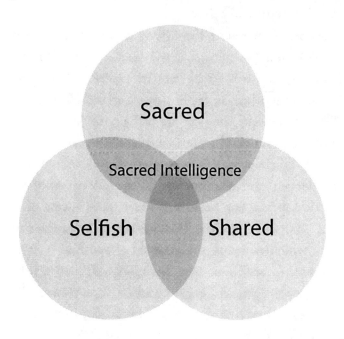

This book is written to help you journey toward *Sacred Intelligence* by reminding some and enlightening others of ways to strengthen our relationships. As each of these relationships is nurtured, we garner the ability to access and use our *Sacred Intelligence*.

I begin with the premise that we must first develop a relationship with the Sacred. I then move into a discussion of the importance of loving ourselves and having a healthy relationship with self. The next section focuses on our shared relationships with others. I conclude with encouraging you to maximize your *Sacred Intelligence*.

Each section begins with a story that illustrates a focus on either a sacred, selfish, or shared relationship. Each chapter begins with a story, primarily a story from Biblical scripture. The stories are not intended to persuade people to hold certain religious beliefs but, rather, are used to engage the reader in examining their patterns of thinking and behaving.

I use stories based on the Christian faith because it is what I know best, and I believe that the stories are highly relevant to teaching others to learn to love the Sacred, themselves, and others. One might just as easily use other sacred texts to teach a similar lesson. Some chapters are to be read with a continuous flow, while others contain a number of sections and bullet points. In some of the chapters, I have included questions designed to help you deepen your relationships in the aforementioned areas. It is my desire that this book will serve as a means of healing for those who find themselves in broken relationships or who have been wounded by past relationships and find it difficult to move forward. I also hope that this book will help you tap into the Sacred within you and begin to make wise choices. You can choose to revive and nurture those relationships which have the potential for manifesting love, joy, and peace. You can choose to change (whenever possible) *or* discard those relationships that are demoralizing, stifling, and overbearing.

Part

I

Sacred
Relationships

Emma's Story

On a very hot and oppressive day in New England, I ventured outside to go to the hair salon. Once outside, I wondered aloud, "Merciful God[3], what am I doing out here?" The answer to that question came later when I was reminded that love, indeed, is a splendid thing. This love was revealed in the story of Emma and those who manifested God's love for her.

Emma was a woman in her 80s who had Alzheimer's disease. This was not the first time that I had seen her at the salon. On several occasions, I had seen her husband, Frank, bring her in, wait patiently, and engage in conversation with the women in the salon. Both his and Emma's appearance and grooming were impeccable, and he treated her with such dignity, caring for her in the most gentle, loving, and kind way. Frank's entire manner exuded love and devotion to Emma. His mannerisms, coupled with his neat self-care and his wife's careful grooming, allowed me to catch a glimpse of their shared relationships.

On this particular day, Frank brought Emma into the salon, guided her to a chair and helped her to sit down. After a brief conversation with the hairstylist, he left Emma to get her hair done. While she waited, Emma sat quietly, staring or nodding, seemingly in another world. Yet, even though it was clear that she had memory loss, Emma seemed to remember God's love for she occasionally would hum a hymn that demonstrated God's love for her and, I believe, her love for God.

Even with memory loss, Emma seemed to remember her deep relationship with God and could show her love and adoration with her heart, soul, strength, and especially her mind, in the best way that she could. Deep down in the core of her very being, she was able to call on God through songs. I imagined that Emma was able to call on a God who had given her strength throughout her life to endure whatever challenges she faced. So, even when Emma might have forgotten the lyrics and could only say "la-la-la-la" to the tune of "Rock of Ages,"[4] her love for God helped her to know that despite cracks and crevices in her memory, she could ask God to shelter her from confusion and fear. She wanted to be completely hidden in God. I believe she understood that no matter her circumstances, she had an intimate relationship with her divine source.

When it was time to do Emma's hair, I witnessed a great example of shared relationships through the actions of her hairstylist. She went over and spoke softly to Emma. She said, "Mrs. Emma, I'm Pam and I'm going to do your hair. Let me help you stand up and walk to the chair."

Mrs. Emma complied but when she got to the chair, she didn't want to sit down, saying to Pam that she was going to fall. Suffice it to say, Mrs. Emma became slightly agitated and moved away from the chair. Pam held her hands the entire time.

"Mrs. Emma," Pam said, "sing me a hymn."

Mrs. Emma said, "I don't remember any songs."

In a very melodious voice, Pam began to sing these words: *"Why should I feel discouraged and why should the shadows come when Jesus is my portion? A constant friend is He. His eye is on the sparrow and I know He watches me."*

Mrs. Emma reached down into the depths of her soul to recall her intimate relationship with the Sacred. She began to sing without fail: "I sing because I'm happy. I sing because I'm free. His eye is on the sparrow and I know He watches me."[5]

Tears welled up in my eyes. I realized in that moment that

Pam's actions did not simply exhibit love for her neighbor nor even her love for God. This was special to witness because many people would have been annoyed and told Frank never to bring Emma back or that he must stay with her. This act was also an example of how—if we develop a relationship with our inner Sacred source and make it the core of our foundation—we can rely on that source for strength, even in our deepest, darkest hour. We do not truly forget. Even when we do not know the words to express our pains or concerns, our Sacred source guides us and seemingly intercedes on our behalf.

1

THE QUIET AND SILENT PLACES

For thus said the Lord God, the Holy One of
Israel: In returning and rest you shall be saved;
in quietness and in trust shall be your strength.

—Isaiah 30:15

The idea of being alone with our own thoughts, let alone with the Sacred, is unsettling and a little scary. We live in a world that perpetuates a *do, do, do* multi-tasking mentality. To take time to rest is considered sacrilegious. We text, make phone calls, take selfies, and post to social media while eating, driving, or walking. We overextend ourselves. In addition to working full-time jobs, we participate in multiple organizations, volunteer in our churches, synagogues, or communities, and spend countless hours running our children from one activity to the next. It is little wonder that we wind up wishing there were more hours in a day. Before our heads hit the pillow, we are out like lights. Truthfully, some of us are asleep while in motion.

We avoid quietness and silence by listening to music, watching TV, playing games on our videos, phones, iPods, etc., or simply talking, texting, or engaging in some other activity on our electronic devices. We are on a path to self-destruction, unable to fully extend ourselves to others or to nurture ourselves, let alone develop, maintain, and rely on a relationship with the Sacred. We have not learned that moments of silence and stillness can open the windows of our minds, hearts, and spirits and inspire us to do even greater things.

In moments when quietness or silence is encouraged, even expected, we are uncomfortable with its presence. Some time ago, I participated in the blessing of a new business and office. As a part of the blessing, one of the facilitators invited us to join in a practice that is typically offered during a Quaker service—to sit in quietness. She asked us to allow the Sacred to engage with us as we pondered some questions. We were asked whether our vocations followed the example of Christ. If the Sacred led, we were to speak from this silence. After only a few moments, a participant spoke. Then there was silence again, but not for long. It seemed evident that some participants were not accustomed to sitting in silence, at least not with a group of people or when directed to do so by someone else.

Not long after this experience, I was reminded how silence can be frightening for some. When fear is involved, we do all that we can to avoid silence. In this case, I had a discussion with a teenager who said she could not study without the TV, computer, and radio going at the same time. She also texted while studying. She said she needed the distraction. My knowledge of her emotional issues made it painstakingly obvious to me—even before she admitted it—that she simply did not want to be alone with her thoughts.

Yet, regardless of age, all of us benefit from moments of quietness. It is important to our spiritual well-being that we find time to be alone and quiet in our thoughts with the Sacred. We may not be actively thinking of the Sacred in the moment but, if we are quiet long enough, we will feel the presence of the Sacred moving and directing our path. We might even be led to that place of purposely seeking the Sacred.

We need those quiet places. For it is in those quiet moments that we find our strength and gain a sense of peace. It is in the quiet moments that we learn to trust the Sacred to see us through our circumstances and to know that we are not alone in our efforts because the Sacred and others are there for us.

Although we may not want to "bother" anyone else, we may be blocking another person's blessing by not allowing them to help. In our quiet places, we gain clarity about the source of our strength. By tapping into that strength, we can accomplish our goals or overcome or endure a particular situation. If we truly rely on and trust the Sacred, we will access the source of our strength to sustain us. In this way, the Sacred often directs us to the people who can help us in our given situation. Consider the following story:

A little boy and his father were walking along a road when they came across a large stone. The boy looked at the stone, seeming to think about it a little. Then he asked his father, "Do you think if I use all my strength, I can move that rock?"

The father thought for a moment and said, "I think that if you use all your strength, you can do it."

That was all the little boy needed. He ran over to the rock and began to push it. He pushed and he pushed. He tried so hard that beads of sweat appeared on his forehead. But the rock didn't move—not an inch, not half an inch.

After a while, the little boy sat down on the ground. His face had fallen. His whole body seemed to be just a lump there on the earth. "You were wrong," he told his dad. "I can't do it."

His father walked over to him, knelt beside him, and put his arm around the boy's shoulders. "You can do it," he said. "You just didn't use all your strength. You didn't ask me to help."[6]

We have the strength we need. We first must be aware that it is available to us. Second, we need only ask the Sacred to give us strength at the appropriate time. When I think back on my days in graduate school, both as a single woman and married, I remember fondly the still, quiet hours between about midnight and 6:00 a.m. Yes, graduate school required long hours; but I felt I could access the Sacred in those long hours. In the stillness, calmness, and quietness, I could hear myself think. More importantly, I was still long enough to allow the Sacred, which lives inside of me, to fully flourish.

It was in those quiet places—when I did not even know how I would begin my papers and dissertation or run another statistical program—that the Sacred would speak. It was in those places that I was able to best utilize what the Sacred had already given and to have strength to continue the long road ahead. These moments were the Sacred in action, helping me to realize that the Sacred has already created the miracle, the blessing and/or the action. Me. This knowledge, belief, and awareness in our sacred selves and the power of the Sacred move us into deeper relationships with others.

Quietness. Silence. Stillness. All lead us to the Sacred.

The Who, What, When and Where of the Sacred

A Constant Friend—When we nurture the Sacred within us, we are able to live our life to the fullest potential. Our awareness of the Sacred deepens the more we open ourselves to the possibility that this source, indeed, exists within us. It is only when we free ourselves of all the reasons why such a source cannot exist and allow ourselves to fully explore its presence that the Spirit will reveal and avail itself to us in our daily lives.

A Vital Source—When we cultivate a Sacred relationship, we are able to cherish our relationships with ourselves. Only then can we learn to fully manifest our unconditional love for another. Without the Sacred relationship, our other relationships will falter. We will find ourselves searching for meaning in life, battling self-destructive behaviors, and attempting to navigate unhealthy interactions with others, such as our spouses, partners, co-workers, etc.

The Benefits of Our Intimate Relationship with the Sacred Are Superb

Peace—An intimate relationship with the Sacred brings a sense of peace. As we confront life's problems, the Sacred helps to center us rather than propel us into a world of worry and confusion. With continued practice, we grow to a place where we think about positive things—those things that are true, kind, pleasing, and worthy. We do not wallow in the negative and pay attention to those voices of fear and anxiety. We learn to release our old patterns of thinking and behaving. We can be secure in the thought that "this too shall pass" when we experience discomfort or a stressful situation.

Assurance—An intimate relationship with the Sacred assures us that we are able to make intelligent choices that will bring about change in our current situation. Even if we are unable to change a particular situation to work in our favor, we can make an intelligent choice regarding how we will deal with the issues surrounding that situation.

Clarity—An intimate relationship with the Sacred will bring clarity about who we are and how we handle situations. If we are reflective and contemplative, we will become aware of those behaviors that promote our well-being and those that deplete our well-being. Once we have a sense of clarity, we can move to a place of change and a commitment to practice those thoughts and behaviors which promote our highest selves.

Self-Worth—An intimate relationship with the Sacred will foster positive self-worth as we learn to accept that we are fearfully and wonderfully created. We begin to embrace that we were created to be good and loving beings who are deserving of loving acts and bountiful blessings. We understand that every instance of pain in our lives is not because we are "bad" or "unlovable" but is related to a myriad of other reasons.

Remembering who we truly are (good and loving individuals) helps us to feel good about ourselves. The Sacred will call us from a place of brokenness to a place of healing when we spend time basking in the presence of the Sacred.

An Intimate Relationship with the Sacred Requires Committed Practice

Standing Appointment—Fostering an intimate relationship requires setting aside time to learn how to tap into the Sacred. In the midst of life's busy demands, setting aside such time may seem impossible. However, starting with just ten minutes a day is an important first step. This time allows us to center ourselves and create a clear space in our minds so that we can "hear" what the Sacred is saying to us.

Familiarity—The more we practice the discipline of spending time with the Sacred, the more we will recognize its prompting, even in the midst of doubt, fear, chaos, or other things that hinder us from embracing life with joy. It is important to push back those uncomfortable feelings and negative thoughts that keep us from dedicating time to commune quietly with our Sacred being.

Inseparable—Beyond our quiet moments, we must also spend time with the Sacred in the mundane and everyday aspects of our lives. We must consciously call to mind that the presence of the Sacred is there to guide and direct our paths, if we observe and listen. If we do, our lives with the Sacred will become so intimate that our decisions are guided by the Sacred; so intentional that our behavior is acceptable to the Sacred; and so interwoven that our will and the Sacred's will become one and the same.

Exercises to Promote Sacred Intimacies

The following exercises will help to foster Sacred intimacies. Each exercise is designed to help you embrace silence and to become a more contemplative listener. While the exercises can be done individually, you will benefit more from incorporating several of them at a time. I invite you to affirm your desire to spend time with the Sacred by repeating the *Sacred Moment* affirmation found at the end of this section.

Preparing to Listen

❧ Create a sacred space within your home that is dedicated to getting in touch with your Sacred being.

❧ Sit in a comfortable position that fosters relaxation but not sleep.

❧ Close your eyes and be conscious of your breathing. Inhale by distending your abdomen. Exhale by pulling in your abdomen. A helpful way to slow down your physiological rate (i.e., heart and pulse) is to breathe in slowly to the count of five, filling and expanding your chest area. Hold your breath for five seconds. Exhale slowly to the count of five, relaxing your shoulders and chest while contracting your abdomen. Do not rush your breathing or your counting. If you take in too much air before you count slowly to five, you will not be able to hold this breath for five counts. Repeat this breath exercise at least three to five times.

❧ Once you have settled and slowed your breathing, continue to be conscious of your breathing but begin to recognize that you are a part of all creation.

❧ As you inhale, imagine yourself being surrounded by the love of your Sacred being. Picture all of your life's concerns drifting away.

❦ Repeat to yourself: *Quietness leads to confidence and strength.*

❦ Offer to the Sacred the thoughts, concerns, and barriers that keep you from wanting to listen. Ask for what you need and listen for the response. The Sacred will only lead you to healthy, whole, and intelligent choices.

Breath Prayer

❦ Sit in a comfortable position with your spine straight and feet on the floor.

❦ Think of a word or phrase that you can divide into two parts (e.g., *The Sacred is near*).

❦ As you inhale, silently say the first part (*The Sacred*), breathing in all that is sacred and good.

❦ As you exhale, silently say the second part (*is near*).

❦ This is your breath prayer. Silently, repeat this phrase continuously. If your mind wanders, guide it back to your breath prayer.

Centering Moments

❦ Sit in a comfortable position with your spine straight and feet on the floor.

❦ If necessary, take several deep breaths to help quiet your spirit. Read a calming phrase or listen to peaceful music to assist you, if you choose.

❦ Choose a word—a positive, hopeful, or confident word—that reminds you that this is your time with the Sacred. Take special care in choosing your word. Try to choose a word with no more than three syllables. Use this word throughout your centering moment.

❦ As you sit in silence in the presence of the Sacred, use this word to guide you back to the Sacred if you become aware of anything else.

❦ The word is not intended to be repeated continuously, as in the breath prayer, but is used to guide you back to the presence of the Sacred, if your mind wanders.

Music Moments

❦ Select music that is calming, peaceful, or inspiring.

❦ Sit in a comfortable position with your spine straight and feet on the floor.

❦ Close your eyes and listen to the music. If it is a familiar tune, try to listen as if you were hearing it for the first time.

❦ Simply allow yourself to be present with the music.

❦ When the music stops, allow yourself to sit in silence for a short time before you transition to your next activity.

Journaling

❦ If possible, dedicate a particular time of day to engage in the practice of journaling.

❦ Find a comfortable and quiet place to sit.

❦ Write anything. Simply write. Allow your deepest thoughts to flow freely onto your pages as you imagine yourself having an intimate conversation with the Sacred.

Reflection Questions

Reflect on your feelings about developing an intimate relationship with the Sacred. Do you believe such a relationship is necessary? Explain. What are your concerns, fears, anxieties, etc.? Record your answers below. Return to them in the coming weeks to see how your answers may change. You can include any new insights in your journaling.

_____

_____

_____

Developing an intimate relationship with the Sacred requires sacrifices (e.g., time). What are you willing to sacrifice, to build, to maintain, and to strengthen your relationship with the Sacred?

_____

_____

_____

Identify three ways that you have nurtured your relationship with the Sacred.

_____

_____

_____

Identify three ways that you have neglected your relationship with the Sacred.

Too busy

To fast overdue

too pushy

Are there specific times or situations in your life when you have not been attentive to this relationship? If so, what steps can you take to ensure that you will dedicate time with the Sacred when similar situations arise?

Make Time — Listen!

Focus —

I think —

When you are experiencing a strong relationship with the Sacred, do you notice differences in . . .

. . . your life circumstances?

. . . your attitude toward life?

_____

_____

_____

. . . your attitude toward others?

_____

_____

_____

Sacred Moment

In the quietness of this moment, I wait for the Sacred.
In the stillness of this moment, I wait for the Sacred.
In the peacefulness of this moment, I wait for the Sacred.
My only petitions are:
To commune with you.
To know you more.
To strengthen my relationship with you.
In the quietness of this moment . . .
In the stillness of this moment . . .
In the peacefulness of this moment . . .
My soul waits for the Sacred.
Come, Sacred, unto me.

—Terrlyn L. Curry Avery

CHAPTER

2

SACRED WORDS AND MEDITATIONS

*Let the words of my mouth and the meditation
of my heart be acceptable in thy sight, O Lord,
my rock and my redeemer.*

—Psalm 19:14

In the previous chapter, the focus was on developing a relationship with the Sacred and understanding the benefits of that relationship. In this chapter, we delve a little deeper into what it means to have such a relationship. What is our response? What is required?

I consider Psalm 19 to be one of David's most beautiful Psalms. His plea in verse 14 expresses his desire that this particular poem—these particular words and thoughts—be acceptable to the Sacred. How does one get to a point where s/he can write anything as beautiful, as pleasing, as acceptable to the Sacred?

It is clear in this verse that both our words and our meditations are necessary to please the Sacred. We cannot simply have one or the other. We must have both. If it were written as a mathematical equation, it would be: Words + Meditations = Acceptable. I believe that one of the things that we learn from this Psalm is that we cannot simply talk to the Sacred or about the Sacred. Instead, we also have to meditate on the Sacred. We have to spend time thinking about things that are acceptable to the Sacred.

For instance, we cannot think solely about how we are going to make our next dollar. We must think about how that dollar might express our understanding of the Sacred and our relationship to others in some way. If we own a business and we ask the Sacred for it to flourish, we must clarify our intention. We can communicate to the Sacred that we want it to flourish not just for ourselves but also for others. If the business succeeds, we might employ others, which allows them to feed themselves and their family members. This way of being lets the Sacred know that we understand our responsibilities to those in need.

Specifically, our minds have to be more in tune with the things of the Sacred, understanding that we do not live in a vacuum but in community with others. When we help others, it benefits us and numerous other people. We begin to understand the African proverb, *Ubuntu*, which is loosely translated "I am because we are." Archbishop Desmond Tutu explained it this way:

> *A person with Ubuntu is open and available to others,*
> *affirming of others, does not feel threatened that others*
> *are able and good, based from a proper self-assurance that*
> *comes from knowing that he or she belongs in a greater*
> *whole and is diminished when others are humiliated or*
> *diminished, when others are tortured or oppressed.*[7]

To be in tune with the Sacred, we cannot spend all of our time listening to music or watching television, filling our minds with all types of useless, unproductive, or distasteful things. We have to balance what we take in with spiritual teachings, with the words of the Sacred, or whatever scriptures or inspirations we use. Think about it. If we spent our time watching nothing but reality shows, we might think it's okay to be completely selfish, rude, overbearing, and heartless. If, however, we meditate on the Sacred's words, we would be reminded that these behaviors have no place in loving one another as we love ourselves. And if we were to put into practice what we see on reality television, neither our words nor our meditations would be acceptable to the Sacred.

The psalm also teaches us that our words and our intentions must be consistent. Have you noticed that in our lives, our intentions and our spoken words do not always match up? We can be thinking about one thing, and something else comes out of our mouths. Sometimes this happens in slightly humorous ways. I have a sister, Anna, who had surgery that required her jaws to be wired closed. After surgery, she looked completely different. Initially, my other sisters and I would simply stare at her but tried not to draw too much attention to the situation. One day, my older sister wanted Anna to get her keys and go to her car to retrieve an item. Rather than saying "Go get my keys," she said, "Go get my teeth." Anna burst into laughter (well, as much as she could with a wired mouth), perplexing my older sister who did not realize her error.

We knew what she meant, but her words were not consistent with her intent. This incident has yielded moments of laughter each time we think of it. So many other times, however, the result can be harmful when our words and intents do not match up. Think about a situation in which you may have called someone the wrong name, and it created a whirlwind of emotions for the other person and overwhelming distress on your part. Such an incident occurred when I mistakenly pronounced the bride and groom as man and wife but used the name of his ex-girlfriend. Clearly, my words did not match my intentions.

This wonderful psalm also makes it clear that it's not enough for the Sacred to be pleased with our words. We can say all of the right things, but it does not mean anything if there is no feeling behind it. Sincerity can sometimes be heard or sensed. Has someone ever apologized to you for something they did that offended you and, for some reason, you simply did not believe they were truly sorry? Or think about someone who seems like the nicest person in the world. That person may say all the right things, but there is something about him or her that does not sit well with you. It could be someone you work with, someone you meet, or it could be a public figure.

A few years ago, there was a candidate running for political office with a flashing smile, good looks, and an ability to wow his audience. When it was revealed that he was unfaithful to his wife, someone I know commented that she was not surprised. Although she could not articulate her reasons, she noted that there was just something about him that she did not trust. In other words, she did not trust that his words matched up with his true heart.

In I Corinthians 13, Paul tells us what this inconsistency means: "If I speak in the tongues of mortals and of angels, but do not have love, I am a noisy gong or a clanging cymbal. Our words mean nothing if they are empty and hollow; they are nothing but noise." Even more importantly, Paul is indicating here that our words mean nothing without the spirit of the Sacred and without our continuous efforts to meditate upon things that are pleasing to the Sacred.

Where our words do not match our intentions, we show no integrity. Our relationship with our spouses has no integrity if we promised "to have and to hold" them, yet we contemplate infidelity with someone else. Our finances have no integrity if we promised to make a payment by the end of the month when we know it might not happen until the end of the year. Our work or

ments have no integrity if we promised to fulfill
bilities when we are unable to because we are
ied.

Now, imagine what our lives would be like if what we said matched what we thought, and what we thought matched what we said. What if we took those words of spiritual inspiration upon which we meditated and spoke them out of our mouths? This action is the launching pad for great achievements.

Imagine if we truly meditated on scriptures such as Hebrews 11:1 "Faith is the substance of things hoped for and the evidence of things unseen." We would begin to think—and to KNOW— that we can accomplish anything we put our minds to. In other words, we would consistently believe the words that we proclaim and act in accordance with the knowledge that the Sacred has already blessed and empowered us to do great things. And we would understand how our meditations and words work together to ultimately shape our destiny. Consider what an unknown author wrote:

Be careful of your thoughts, because your thoughts become words.

Be careful of your words, because your words become actions.

Be careful of your actions, because your actions become habits.

Be careful of your habits, because your habits become your destiny.

Thoughts! Words! Actions! Habits! Destiny! It is important that our thoughts match up with what is in our hearts; and they will match up with our hearts when we are able to meditate on good things.

We might not find it easy to align our words with our meditations. With practice comes change—a new way of thinking and a new way of behaving. There are times that we have to say things until we get to the point of believing them. For instance, when I am trying to help someone build their self-worth, I often give them mirror exercises that require them to make positive statements while looking in the mirror. Initially, they often do not believe the words. Saying them feels false and forced. However, if they keep repeating the words, they reach a point where they believe, where the positive affirmation becomes more true for them than the negative feelings they previously held. Their perception of themselves changes, unlike people who simply speak words to make themselves look good or to make someone else feel better, either because they do not want to be bothered or are simply being hypocritical.

When we practice words that uplift us and help us to understand that we are made in the image of the Sacred, we purposefully bring our hearts into line with our words. Through these exercises, we will naturally be brought to an awareness and an examination of our hearts to explore the inconsistencies between our hearts and minds. It is at this point that we are consciously expressing a desire for something different.

This powerful verse helps us to see the importance of meditating on the Sacred's words, so that our own words can be more acceptable. It speaks to the importance of being consistent in our words and the deep meditations of our hearts. If we go a little further, I believe that this verse also tells us that the Sacred wants us to be consistent in our prayers to and communication with the Sacred.

In other words, be transparent with the Sacred and acknowledge what we are really feeling. If we are angry with the Sacred because we believe the Sacred did not hold to a promise, express that emotion. I am not necessarily saying that we would be justified in our anger; we could be blaming the Sacred for something that is not the Sacred's fault. It is, however, important to at least express that anger to the Sacred.

Unexpressed anger can lead to resentment and, inevitably, behaviors that are inconsistent with our words, as well as behaviors that are self-destructive and demoralizing to others in our path. We cannot say one thing because we think it is the right thing to do when we know in our hearts we are angry with the Sacred. Remember, both our words and our meditations—not just our words—have to be acceptable to the Sacred.

Our current situation might not change immediately, but we must begin to trust the Sacred enough to be truthful in expressing the desires of our hearts. This process of truth telling and trust may feel false and forced like the mirror exercises mentioned above. With practice, however, it begins to feel more natural, and we learn to share with the Sacred as we would a dear friend. If we are able to tell the Sacred what is deep within our hearts, we can begin to ask the Sacred to heal our hearts of brokenness. We can ask the Sacred to change our hearts so that it will be consistent with the Sacred's desire for us. And when our words and meditations are consistent, we will be profoundly blessed. The Sacred wants the very best for us. May the words of our mouths and the meditations of our hearts be acceptable in the Sacred's sight, so that we might have all the riches of life that the Sacred desires for us.

3

SACRED SERENITY

*B*ret is a recovering alcoholic who has been sober for 18 years but who also suffers from severe anxiety. At times, he has great difficulty controlling his thoughts and his worries. He worries that he might one day drink again. He worries that he is not as smart as people think and worries that he might be asked to do something of which he is incapable.

Bret's anxiety affects his sleep. He worries about how he will function when he goes on a trip with a group of people, when he's in a large family gathering, when he gets his hair cut, or when he has to talk to others in social situations. He worries about the most minor details when he's working on a project. He worries to the point of exhaustion, depression, and sometimes paralysis. Bret worries! But when he is at his best, he remembers one of the principles of Alcoholics Anonymous—to let go and to rely on the Sacred to settle his thoughts. He remembers to say a portion of the Serenity Prayer.

God grant me the serenity to accept the things I cannot change,
The courage to change the things that I can,
And the wisdom to know the difference.

Bret is not unlike many of us. We worry. We worry. We worry! Some of us may not have a severe anxiety disorder, but we worry. We worry about the meeting that we have to prepare for tomorrow. We worry about the right outfit to wear to work, to a function, or to meet someone special. We worry about our health. We worry about the house, the finances, the children or other family members. We worry about how we are going to meet all of the demands in life. We worry about our past. We worry about our present. We worry so much about the future that we cannot even enjoy the present. But I believe that one of the cures for our worries is found in a portion of The Serenity Prayer.

God grant me the serenity to accept the things that I cannot change . . .

Radical Acceptance—There are many areas in our lives that we are unable to change. We cannot change the fact that we performed poorly on a school project. We cannot change the fact that someone's feelings might have been hurt by our actions. We cannot change our lack of resources at this moment. We cannot change our spouses' or our own infidelity or lack of attention. We cannot change the decisions of those in authority. We cannot change the medical diagnoses that we have been given. The list goes on.

Because we cannot change many of the circumstances of our lives, we must be in a place that Dr. Tara Brach calls radical acceptance. She says: "The way out of our cage begins with accepting absolutely everything about ourselves and our lives, by embracing with wakefulness and care our moment-to-moment experience." In other words, we accept the situation as it is.

As Brach explains, acceptance does not mean that we resign ourselves to the situation, become passive, or accept whatever the limitations might be. It does, however, require us to be in a place where we accept what is happening in that experience and begin to see clearly where we are in the present. We are in a place that does not allow us to emotionally batter ourselves about the situation, but we can—simply and with compassion—acknowledge where we are in the process. What radical acceptance does, according to Brach, is to help us "acknowledge our own experience in the moment as the first step in wise action."[8]

We can only move ahead once we accept where we are and who we are in the current moment. Even if we are an alcoholic, drug addict, abusive person, workaholic, passive-aggressive person; even if we are depressed, anxious, uptight, or rude, we can move forward to healing when we acknowledge our state of being. Once we accept who we are, it will open the door to changes, both internally and externally, that will impact our life in a more positive way.

Radical Solutions—Accepting where we are opens the door for radical solutions. When we acknowledge our circumstances, we begin to move from a place of dwelling in our emotional bondage to a place of freedom. We can then begin to see the alternative to our situation. We no longer deny or continuously focus on the problem. Rather, we can begin to target those behaviors that need changing, restructure our negative thoughts, and position ourselves for radical transformation, which may include going against the norm.

The courage to change the things I can . . .

Stepping Outside of the Box—As powerful as radical acceptance and radical solutions are, they are most effective when we have the courage to move in the direction of change and to step outside of the box. Our decision to change our lives or to heal our current circumstances can be hampered by the barriers we put into place as well as confined rules (perceived or real) of friends, family, or society. We must have the courage to move beyond these constraints and not be consumed by someone else's expectations of what is right for us. We must have courage to speak up and ask for help to overcome our problems. The courage does not end with the asking for assistance nor with the generation of solutions, but it must encompass action.

Action—Taking active steps requires courage and is necessary in order for our healing or change to take place. In my role as a psychologist, I often encounter people who do not want to take medication for some of their problems (e.g., ADHD, depression, anxiety, etc.). People with a strong belief in the Sacred, in particular, will often say that they do not want to take medication because they believe that the Sacred will heal them. Many of these individuals do not want to come to therapy for that same reason. Undoubtedly, some people are healed by the miraculous power of the Sacred! The truth of the matter, however, is the healing power of the Sacred often comes through other means, such as a psychologist or medications. The Sacred has had a hand in the creation of the medications and in bestowing gifts or talents to individuals that allow them to become therapists. The Sacred wants us, through prayer and supplications, to be courageous enough to use the tools that are available and, perhaps, sent to us by the Sacred.

Restructuring Our Thoughts—The courage to step outside of the box and move into action often requires restructuring our thoughts. We cannot allow our limited thinking to prohibit us from seeking help from an unlikely source. It takes courage for us to recognize that sometimes our help might come from someone we least expect. Sometimes, we have to let go of the disdain that we have for others and ask for their help. We have to let go of thoughts about how they might react, what they might say or what others might think. It takes courage to let go of our pride, our self-righteousness, our bitterness, our hatred, or our anger. We can change the course of so many situations if we just have the courage to change our thinking and let go of the thoughts that bind us.

The wisdom to know the difference.

Recognize the Problem—Before we can ask the Sacred to help us accept the things we cannot change, give us the courage to change the things that we can, and show us the difference between the things that we cannot change, we must first recognize that we have a problem. Some time ago, I was treating Mike and Linda, a couple in therapy. They had been in therapy for about a year when I decided to do a check-in to evaluate how they felt about their progress and to explore what changes they saw in themselves and in their marriage. In response to this inquiry, Mike boldly stated that he did not have any problems. He had only been coming to therapy the entire time to help Linda work on her problems. Needless to say, Linda was not very happy and her choice words in the response alerted Mike to her hurt and anger. It was not until I took a different course of action to get Mike to examine some very specific things about himself and his views regarding relationships that he began to realize that he did have a few problems. Mike could address his problems only after recognizing he had problems.

Believe Change Is Possible—Many of us might recognize that we have a bit of a problem in certain areas but think, "Oh that's just the way I am. I cannot change it. I don't need to change it." Worse yet, we view the situation as daunting. We think, "It's all over now. I cannot change. I have been this way for years." For instance, Bret remembers being anxious as a child and growing up in a home where his parents physically fought a lot. He began to drink to cover up his anxiety and to deal with his problems at home. When he was older, he found employment, left home, joined the military, and continued to drink and to engage in other activities excessively. Once married, his drinking continued but he was able to function on the job. Of course, the drinking eventually began to impact all areas of his life. Bret first did what most people with problems do. He said those famous words, "I don't have a problem." And he began to blame everyone else around him rather than looking at himself. When his position within his organization began to be threatened and he was ordered to get help for his drinking, he accepted that he had a problem but doubted that he could overcome it or that he could face life without the aid of alcohol.

When we are used to doing something every day of our lives, it becomes a habit, a part of our very beings. The action is almost automatic, and we find ourselves doing it without thinking. When something is so ingrained in us that we are not even conscious of when we are doing it, fear grips us if we are suddenly asked to change it. It is overwhelming. And when that habit is something like alcoholism, detoxing affects us physically. It can be unbearable. We believe it is not possible to change and we resign ourselves to stay in our situations. If we ask, the Sacred will grant us wisdom to know what areas of our lives we have the power to change. Changing one area of our lives leads to changes and vast improvements in other parts of our lives, and we move toward wholeness and completeness.

CHAPTER 4

SURVIVING THE PERFECT STORM

He woke up and rebuked the wind, and said to the sea, 'Peace! Be still!' Then the wind ceased, and there was a dead calm.

—Mark 4:39

In life, we are often confronted with challenging and stormy situations. Sometimes, these challenges come to us "out of the blue." Other times, they coalesce into the perfect storm. A perfect storm is a combination of events that are not individually dangerous but, occurring together, they produce a disastrous outcome. Often, following a tragedy such as a public display of violence—particularly one that involves a high-profile individual or multiple people at one time, or an act of nature that causes severe flood damage and loss of lives—news analyses will describe these situations as the perfect storm. Review of the events helps to reveal how important it is to consider even seemingly small and innocent events or occurrences that might contribute to devastating consequences.

49

Like any public and global storms, there are, at times, perfect storms that brew in our lives. There are situations in our lives that we find we are able to handle individually but when they begin to occur together, they become waves that are fierce and strong. Such waves seem to knock us down even before we are standing on solid ground—waves that have us begging for safety and waves that might make us wonder if the Sacred even exists or is there for us. In the midst of these storms, the possibility of survival may seem daunting but the tools to survive these perfect storms are readily available to us, especially if we tap into the Sacred. If we take into consideration and put into practice the recommended activities and the discussions in the previous chapters, we will be able to survive the storms of our lives.

Be Still and Remain Calm

When we find ourselves battling the storms of life, we have a variety of ways we respond. Some of us respond by trying to control everything, falsely believing that if we are managing our circumstances, the end result will be just as we hope. Some of us believe that we have all the answers and do not need to consult anyone else to resolve the problem. Many of us respond with anxiety, fear, and sadness. Our brains are working a mile a minute, even if our bodies are not. Others of us forget to call on the Sacred, even when we have a strong sense that the Sacred is there for us.

Taking the time to be still and call upon the Sacred for direction is an extremely important step toward surviving our storms. Students of sacred text are likely aware of scriptures that proclaim victory and peace when the Sacred intervenes in our lives. If we sit still long enough when chaos presents itself as storms upon a sea, we realize that there are many situations in our lives that we are unable to control. If we sit still, we begin to recognize that there is a power greater than ourselves that can calm the stormy seas of life that we face every day. When we still ourselves, we have an opportunity to grow in the Sacred, to learn to rely on the Sacred and to trust that the Sacred will prevail. It is in these moments that we let go of anxiety, even for the "big things" in life. We refrain from thinking about all the negative aspects of our situation and begin to think about whatever is hopeful, positive, admirable, and necessary. If we do so, there is a peace given to us by the Sacred that will guard our hearts.

Use the Tools in Your Possession

By now, you have gotten the concept that when we "be still" and acknowledge the Sacred, we are able to hear the Sacred speaking clearly and can figure out what tools, skills, or gifts we have to help us through the situation. It is important for us to have that time of sitting still to look at the situation from all sides and consider the various methods of tackling the problem.

Let us look at a familiar story from not only a sacred text but one that has been "brought to life" by Hollywood. It is the story of Moses and the people of Israel at the Red Sea, with water in front of them and Pharaoh and his army pursuing them. Despite having a staff in his hand that had performed many miracles and despite his verbalization to the people that God would fight for them if they only be still, Moses must have cried out to God. The answer comes in Exodus 14:15 which reads: "Then the Lord said to Moses, 'Why do you cry out to me? Tell the Israelites to go forward. But you lift up your staff, and stretch out your hand over the sea and divide it, that the Israelites may go into the sea on dry ground." In today's language I imagine God saying to Moses: "I got your back." "Don't stand there crying." "Go!"

Some of us want to just sit back and let the Sacred do all the work, even though the Sacred has clothed us in our right minds. We would rather wait for someone else to tell us what to do. For some of us, the Sacred has even sent others into our lives to direct us, but we do not want to accept their help out of pride. We do not want to share our business with others, not realizing that others are going through situations similar to our own. At other times, God has endowed us with resources. Yet, when we need help, we do not want to receive it because we deem it too expensive or would rather spend our money on other things that are not crucial to our lives or well-being.

We cannot let fear, despair, hopelessness, busyness, and a plethora of other reasons prohibit us from using these tools. Nor can we wait around expecting that the Sacred will do everything for us, believing that we are acting faithfully by "letting go and letting God." Surely, there is a time for letting go, but there is clearly a time to act. Faith without action is futile. The Sacred does not micromanage our lives. We have been created in the Sacred's image and are endowed with power to function in this earthly realm.

Stand Firm

When we are still and wait for guidance from the Sacred and use the tools we have been given, then we can stand firm. We stand firm when we proceed with caution, move forward as necessary, and step out on the assurance that all will be well, regardless of the outcome. We stand still and see the Sacred moving in us and also in the lives of others. Whether our circumstances change immediately or never, we feel victorious and move through our lives with a sense of inexplicable serenity. The storms of life can be overwhelming and unbearable at times, but our reliance on the Sacred will help us to survive. Consequently, it is important for us to consistently stay in the presence of the Sacred in good and bad times. It is particularly important to recall the times that the Sacred has helped us to overcome life's challenges or sustained us in the midst of such challenges. We are survivors of our storms. Otherwise, we would not be reading this book now. We have everything we need!

SELFISH RELATIONSHIPS

Rebecca's Story

In July of 2013, I was going through a divorce, seeing clients as well as managing my psychological practice alone (after my part-time assistant took a full-time position), adjusting to an altogether different and challenging financial terrain, nursing my baby, and caring for my two dogs. I was, in a word, overwhelmed. In fact, I felt like I was tenuously holding up a mountain that continued to grow.

One morning, as I prepared for work, I lay down on the floor of my closet and I just wanted to remain there. I called a friend and I told her that we had to get away immediately, that I felt that I was at a breaking point. She expressed concern and encouraged me to not go into work that day. I told her that I was able to go into work but that I realized I really needed a break. She indicated that she and her child could get away in the next two to three weeks.

The universe provided for me and I found an inexpensive ticket to visit my relatives on the East Coast. Within a week and a half, my divorce was finalized and my son and I headed to the East Coast for about ten days. Leaving my practice is always difficult for me. If I do not work, I do not get paid. Still, I knew that I would not be any use to anyone if I continued the way that I had been going. Thus, I gave my clients notice of my leave, along with emergency contact information, and I packed my bags. I made the decision to take care of me and to do something that was nourishing for me, even though some may have viewed it as hasty or unnecessary. I was overwhelmed by the demands of running my practice alone. I was overwhelmed by the demands of being a single mother. I knew that I needed a respite and some assistance immediately. Before I left for my trip, I told my family that I did not want to make a decision about a single thing while I was away.

While away, I accepted help and allowed myself to be revitalized and rejuvenated by being in the presence of those who loved and cared for me and my child. I took time to read, to sit outside and simply revel in nature. I took time to relax. I saw a Broadway play. I played with my son without regard for time, schedules, or the next task awaiting completion. I took time to have fun. I happily let family members care for my son while I took time for myself. It was just what I needed, just what the doctor ordered, and the very best gift that I and my family could have given me at that time.

5

BE SELFISH

> *In the morning, while it was still very dark, he got up and went out to a deserted place, and there he prayed.*
>
> —Mark 1:35

The word selfish, by its very definition, implies something negative. To be selfish means that one is only concerned about his/her own well-being, without consideration for others. For many, the word selfish in relationship to oneself creates discomfort. Undoubtedly, readers will feel uneasy with its use and wonder why another word was not chosen instead. Frankly speaking, there are times that we need to be selfish. Selfish intimacy means spending time with self. So many individuals spend time taking care of other folks' needs that little time is left to care for themselves. It is important to take time out and learn how to say "no."

"No" is a powerful word to have in our vocabulary in order to develop selfish intimacy. If we say "yes" to everything we are asked to do, it can leave us depleted, irritable, and often angry. As a result, our interactions with others may be less patient and more resentful.

Consequently, a lack of selfish intimacy can lead to interactions and relationships with others that are destructive. If we do not spend time with ourselves and with the Sacred, we are not able to determine what our needs are or express them to others. Sometimes, this leads to engaging in behaviors and activities that others impose, even at the risk of harm to ourselves. Rather than falling into these traps, take a little time to be selfish.

Being Selfish Can Be a Good Thing

Heart's Desire—Selfishness promotes uncovering and nurturing our dreams and hearts' desires in ways that will allow us to use our gifts and talents to benefit ourselves and others. When we are alone we have an opportunity to focus our attention on us if we dedicate this space for our hearts' desires, rather than the desires of others. We can ask the questions, "What do I really want in life? What are my passions? What brings me joy?"

Healthy Well-being—If we give everything we have to others, we "end up in the same boat" as they are and can no longer help them or ourselves. For instance, if we spend all of our time taking care of everyone else, we become "run down" and perhaps ill and unable to meet life's daily demands. Taking time to care for ourselves is crucial to promoting a healthy well-being.

Greater Capacity to Love—Our ability to fully share who we are with others is manifested when we demonstrate love for ourselves. It is only when we take the opportunity to dedicate time for self-renewal and rejuvenation and to express our needs clearly to others that we are able to exhibit unconditional love and acceptance of others. Time with ourselves helps us to avoid irritability, resentment, anger, and frustration from being pulled in too many directions. Loving ourselves enough to create selfish moments sends a message to others that we value ourselves just as we value them.

Self-Examination Is a Necessity for Selfish Intimacy

Reasons Why—Self-examination allows for an opportunity to explore reasons why we do not take time for ourselves. It requires us to take an in-depth look at our patterns of behavior and to determine whether there is a reason we do not spend time with ourselves. For instance, do we say "yes" to others out of a sense of guilt, shame, responsibility, etc.? Do we avoid spending time with ourselves because we do not like who we are?

Feelings—Self-examination will help us to explore our own feelings of self-worth and to understand more deeply how we relate to the world around us. It is an opportunity to explore how our history impacts the present and how we can change future patterns of behavior.

Exercises to Promote Selfish Intimacy

The following exercises are offered to facilitate a greater understanding of who you are, what your needs are, and what changes in behavior patterns are necessary for your psychological, social, and emotional well-being.

Basking in the Self

❦ Make a list of all the things that you love to do (or loved to do before you became too absorbed with life's responsibilities). Look at that list and determine how many of those things you find time to do. Commit to finding time to engage in those activities.

❦ Get a small hand-held mirror, old magazines, scissors, and tape. Look through the magazine and pick out positive words that describe you, your dreams, and your gifts. Cut these words out and tape them to the perimeter of your mirror. Every time you look in the mirror, remind yourself of the great person you are and the goals you have for yourself.

❦ Make a list of five positive things about yourself and repeat them to yourself daily while looking in the mirror. Be sure to really look at yourself while engaging in this activity.

Imagination Makes It Possible

Get a blank sheet of paper (preferably without lines). Look at the blank paper and create a story that has a beginning, middle, and end that describes your ideal life. Make sure that you describe how you and each of the characters in the story feel. Now, what do you need to do to make this story a reality?

The Tough Stuff: *Exploring Your Self-Worth*

❦ Make a list of those behaviors that are self-destructive or that promote unhealthy choices. This list will help you to recognize problematic areas that require intervention.

❦ Once you have made the list, generate a list of alternative positive behaviors and decide which one or two of those behaviors you can begin to implement immediately. Then set a date for when the other positive behaviors will be implemented.

❦ Seek therapeutic intervention if changing these patterns of behavior is too overwhelming to do alone.

Reflection Questions

❧ How do you feel when you say "no" to others? Why do you feel this way? Is it something that you want to change? If so, how can you begin to change?

_____

_____

_____

❧ What are some ways that you nurture your relationship with yourself?

_____

_____

_____

❧ How do you feel about your own self-worth? (e.g., What is the history of your self-worth? What are some of the negative messages that you have received in the past from family, intimate partners, friends, and even from yourself?)

_____

_____

_____

❦ How do these feelings and thoughts impact your daily living (e.g.,
your choice of romantic partners or what you allow to happen in
your relationships)?

_____

_____

_____

❦ How do these feelings and thoughts interfere with the Sacred's
plan(s) for you?

_____

_____

_____

CHAPTER **6**

TAKE CHARGE OF YOUR HEALING

*N*ow he was teaching in one of the synagogues on the sabbath. And just then there appeared a woman with a spirit that had crippled her for eighteen years. She was bent over and was quite unable to stand up straight. When Jesus saw her, he called her over and said, 'Woman, you are set free from your ailment.' When he laid his hands on her, immediately she stood up straight and began praising God. But the leader of the synagogue, indignant because Jesus had cured on the sabbath, kept saying to the crowd, 'There are six days on which work ought to be done; come on those days and be cured, and not on the sabbath day.' But the Lord answered him and said, 'You hypocrites! Does not each of you on the sabbath untie his ox or his donkey from the manger, and lead it away to give it water? And ought not this woman, a daughter of Abraham whom Satan bound for eighteen long years, be set free from this bondage on the sabbath day?' When he said this, all his opponents were put to shame; and the entire crowd was rejoicing at all the wonderful things that he was doing.*

–Luke 13:10-17

Spirits That Can Cripple Us

Few people experience life without experiencing something that weighs them down or that prohibits them from moving forward in an unencumbered manner. These experiences become such a part of our lives that they are crippling spirits. These spirits take on many forms and manifest themselves in many ways. They are such a part of our daily lives and our core being that we accept them as though they were naturally a part of our original design just as, say, the color of our skin, eyes, or hair.

We often cannot pinpoint when these spirits became infused with our nature and often do not recognize that they are crippling. Some of these spirits manifest themselves psychologically, such as anxiety, stress, discord, anger, fear, hopelessness, depression, resentment, or low self-esteem. Other spirits are emotional, such as impatience, frustration, or irritability. Still others are socially constructed, such as discomfort for those who look differently, love differently, think differently, or act differently. These spirits impact how we behave and respond to each other. Unlike physically crippling spirits, these other crippling spirits, in some cases, are not readily apparent to other people nor are they apparent to us.

Some Crippling Spirits Can Be Long Lasting

Our lack of awareness can result in some crippling spirits being long lasting. Even when we are aware that there is something crippling us, our mindset can contribute to our inability to be healed from these impediments. For instance, we can engage in faulty thinking such as: "That's just the way I am." "I'm too old to change." "I can't do anything about it." "It runs in the family." Such thoughts, especially those that are unconscious or that are in our subconscious, cause us to engage in self-destructive or stagnating behaviors.

In our quiet moments and when we are focused on our healing, some of us pray or meditate on our healing. When we are not led to take the action steps we desire or when the healing process takes longer than we expected, we give up or try half-heartedly to change. Without commitment or a willingness to open ourselves to multiple ways of healing, our crippling spirits last longer. These spirits also persist longer when we refuse to believe that we are the ones who hold the key to our healing. We delay healing when we believe instead that we must rely on an outside source or wait for divine intervention from the Sacred.

Some Crippling Spirits Can Bend Us

When we are weighted down by crippling spirits, they can have us bent over and unable to stand up straight. Many people who are bent over tend to look at the ground. It requires more effort to look straight ahead or upward. All that is available to the observer is what can be seen in the near vicinity.

When we look up, however, our vision is broader. We are able to see not only what is in front of us but what lies in the distance. We can see what is blocking or may potentially block our path, as well as the various avenues to a clear pathway. Most assuredly, we are better able to see and envision the possibilities because our vision is not narrowed by our limited view or circumstances.

The Sacred Calls Each of Us to Be Healed

By nature, we are meant to be whole and healthy beings. We were created in a sacred image and declared good, indicating that we are not meant to live downtrodden and in despair.

When we are crippled by a spirit, the Sacred wants each of us to be healed. Our healing is not necessarily being free of our afflictions but free of the attitudes, thoughts, and feelings that hold us captive and prevent us from experiencing an abundant life. If we examine closely the story of Jesus healing the crippled woman in the temple, we will see that Jesus' actions demonstrate an invitation to everyone to be healed. For instance, the mere fact that he spoke to and touched a woman during a time when Jewish men did not speak to or touch women in public indicated that healing is for all genders and suggested that none of us is more important than anyone else. Further, the healing of her crippling spirit suggested that she was not being punished by the Sacred for anything that she had done. Sometimes, bad things happen to good people.

We Must Respond to This Calling

We cannot be healed unless we respond to opportunities for healing. We are co-creators with the Sacred. We must actively do our part to live a healthier, happier, and healed life. There are multiple reasons we do not take advantage of these opportunities. Sometimes, we are frightened by how our lives would change as a result of healing. Other times, we do not want to dig up old wounds or confront traumatic situations that have crippled us. At other times, we are hesitant because we want to follow the rules or the expectations of others.

What if the woman had not responded to Jesus because it was against the rules to talk to him in public or to be healed on the Sabbath? Sometimes, we need to go against the grain. What if the psychological healing we need is to see a therapist, but our cultural beliefs tell us that we are weak if we do? We must be able to respond as the Sacred directs. The Sacred is calling each of us and we must respond by breaking out of the box and declaring that we are ready to be healed.

Healing Can Occur Anytime, Anywhere, and by Any Means

We often have rules, guidelines, or expectations for when our healing can take place. Not so with the Sacred; the unexpected occurs with the Sacred. In our story, Jesus healed on the Sabbath, the holy day, demonstrating the Sacred's compassion and love for us and declaring that our healing can take place anytime or anywhere. We must be open to the possibilities of healing and expect it to occur anytime, anywhere, and by any means, even in the midst of destructive behavior. For instance, a former drug user once shared with me that he was in the midst of getting high when the Sacred said to him, "How long do you think I can keep saving you?" This was his wake-up call that he needed to get help to change his life and be healed. When we avail ourselves to the Sacred, the pathway to our healing opens up. We must look for it and expect it at every turn in the road.

There Is Healing in the Presence of the Sacred

Dedicated time with the Sacred allows us to be focused and not be distracted by the influences of others. Spending fifteen minutes a day in a listening mode—not asking, speaking, or pleading—can dislodge brain blockage. In other words, the Sacred has room to move unencumbered by outside influences, pause for a minute or two in certain corners of our minds, and direct our steps with clarity. While time alone with the Sacred is powerful, being with others in the presence of the Sacred can be equally powerful, particularly when it is with a faith community that shares a similar belief system. These individuals, with the help of the Sacred, may offer wise counsel, suggest support resources, or simply be a source of personal support as you are healing.

Our Healing Impacts Others

Our healing demands that we honor and acknowledge the Sacred. We are co-creators in our healing and can do nothing without the Sacred's help. When we openly acknowledge the Sacred and proclaim our healing, others begin to see the changes in us. They not only begin to respond to us differently but also wonder how they can be healed and how they can become more connected with the Sacred. There is virtually very little that we do in life that does not in some way impact others—good or bad.

Exercises and Reflection

❧ Take a moment to think about consistent feedback you have received from others regarding your thoughts, behaviors, or patterns. Make a list by writing down a few words that would summarize this feedback.

_____

_____

_____

❧ Look over your list of "spirits." Which of these "spirits" impact your life or others? How can you take charge and be healed of your "spirits?"

_____

_____

_____

CHAPTER

7

IT'S TIME TO CLEAN YOUR HOUSE

A clean house is a sign of a misspent life.

—Unknown

I am not sure exactly what this person had in mind when making this statement. I imagine that the statement implies that if we are spending time cleaning our houses, we are not having too much fun. We are not enjoying life to the fullest. On the other hand, it could also mean that we are not inventing the next great thing to advance human nature. Perhaps all of these things are true. Maybe that is why some people pay other people to clean their homes for them. If we think about it, however, even when someone else cleans for us, there is a bit of pre-cleaning that must be done so that the cleaning service can do what they need to do.

Regardless of who is doing the cleaning, there comes a time when everyone's house has to be cleaned. In some cases, our houses have become cluttered, filthy, and down-right dangerous to live in. They have gotten to a place where it is difficult for us to see the light of day. Some of us are so consumed by so much stuff that we cannot even feel, see, or be reminded that the Sacred resides in our houses. Of course, I am not simply talking about the houses in which we live. I am talking about the houses of our minds and our spirits that are so cluttered with the ways of the world that we can only see a glimpse of the Sacred and the divinity in ourselves and others.

In Order for Us to Clean House, We Must Recognize It Needs Cleaning

Gradual Takeover—We can get so used to mess, filth, dishonesty, and bad habits that they become acceptable, even though it does not start out that way. For instance, it starts with a few clothes on the floor, then a mound of clothes in the corner or on the chair in our rooms that is supposed to be for sitting purposes. Before we know it, we get so used to having the mess that it no longer bothers us when we walk in the room. We just look over it and, in some people's cases, they even step over it or walk around it. A similar process happens with our negative thoughts and/or destructive behaviors.

Questionable Relationships—The need to clean our houses is also analogous to other areas in our lives that need cleaning. Take a moment to think about some of the friendships and associates you have or have had. Often, we are taught to have certain standards and beliefs but may form relationships with people who have beliefs that are drastically different from our own. In general, there is nothing wrong with forming such relationships. We should welcome different views because it can open us up to wonderful experiences. We must exercise caution, however, when we begin to spend time with people who do some questionable things, those who have us questioning our morals and ethics, and advocating actions with which we are initially uncomfortable. If we are not careful, we may become so used to other people's views that they no longer look questionable.

Risky Behaviors—We begin to rationalize behaviors that we previously considered unethical or amoral. We might say to ourselves, "It's okay to borrow money from petty cash. John does it." "I don't need to report all of my income on this form; I really need all the help I can get." Likewise, we rationalize behaviors that can lead to destructive habits or addictions. For instance, we might say to ourselves that it's okay to smoke a little pot. What happens, however, when that behavior interferes with our ability to make sound judgments or if it graduates to something more serious? Do we become so used to the instant gratification that a high, buzz, or intoxication can give us that we no longer recognize that our houses are beginning to overflow with destructive behaviors and patterns that seek to destroy our sacred bodies?

We Must Recognize the Danger of Not Cleaning the House

Hazardous to Our Health—At the first sign that something is not right in our lives, we must get moving. What happens when we do not clean our houses? Dust begins to collect. Mildew begins to surface. Fungus begins to grow. For some people, junk begins to pile so high and wide that there are only small spaces to move around the area or room. All of these things are hazardous to our health. Think for a moment about the harmful effects of mold and mildew. Think about the disease and devastation that can result from an infestation of bugs. Think about the emotional toll on a hoarder of collecting but, especially, of getting rid of things that have helped them in some way reduce their anxiety or satisfy some other emotional issue. Typically, they fail to identify the root cause of these issues or to seek counseling to reduce the anxiety and/or resolve the problem(s).

Blinded by the Old—The danger in not cleaning our house is that we cannot make room for new things—those things that will help to make our living easier, more pleasant and more enjoyable. If we do not recognize the dangers, when we bring the new things in, they just get swept up with the old. They all look the same and we cannot appreciate any of them. Likewise, if we are making changes in our lives and they are overshadowed by a hundred other things that are potentially more dangerous, the new changes are a small surface of cleaning in the midst of the pile of filth that prevents us from living and loving an abundant life.

Paralyzed by Embarrassment—Another danger in not cleaning our house is we become embarrassed by its state. In our lives, we are embarrassed by things that have happened to us (e.g., physical, sexual, or emotional abuse). Sometimes we can hold on to things that depress us, which makes us want to keep other people out of our lives. At other times, we do not want to trust people based on looks, race, gender, class, or political affiliation. Yet, we have to learn to clean mistrust out of our lives and begin to experience the love of the Sacred in a fresh new way through our new and positive experiences with others. The Sacred blesses us as we learn to let go of all things that have held us captive or in bondage. It is imperative that we move beyond the embarrassment and begin a thorough cleaning. This cleaning process may take a while but will ultimately move us forward in life.

We Must Recognize the Urgency of Cleaning Our House

Clean Below the Surface—When we have things that weigh us down emotionally, psychologically, and spiritually, we cannot continue to put aside cleaning those things out of our minds. We must begin to clean with some intensity and purpose. We must use our frustration, intolerance, and anger as a driving force for healing, rather than as a weapon of destruction. It is crucial that we clean below the surface. If we clean the surface only, our problems return a lot sooner, and we have not gotten to the root of them.

Permanent Removal—We cannot get rid of one or two negative thoughts or friends that are bringing us down. We must do some intensive cleaning to get rid of all that is negative. Think for a moment: If we do not like to be around women who talk about other women, we must turn them loose, especially if they do not change after we tell them that we do not like hearing such things. If we do not like being around men who say disrespectful things about their wives or other women, we must clean them out of our lives. When people, circumstances, thoughts, or behaviors prohibit us from having a clean mind, spirit, and life, we must remove them permanently.

Benefits of a Clean House

Open Space—Cleaning our houses allows us to move through it more freely, unencumbered by the clutter that either blocks, distracts, or immobilizes us. The clean houses of our minds allows the Sacred to move within us. We can begin to see the Sacred more clearly in ourselves and in others. Why? Because we have opened up space. We have de-cluttered that part of our brain that only allow us to think about the list of things we have to do, the bills we have to pay, the troubles we are going through, the loved one we must take care of, or the myriad things for which we are responsible.

When we clean our sacred houses (us), we create a sacred space within us that allows us to know that we are worth more than our bank accounts; than our performance on the job or on other tasks in our lives; worth more even than our strongest quality or characteristic (e.g., being a giver). When we clean our houses, we are able to create space for others in our lives who we may have neglected or perhaps have never taken the time to find because we were too busy.

New Possibilities—When we clean our houses, it opens up a whole new set of possibilities. Most of us can think for a moment about a messy drawer or a messy corner or a messy room that we have in our houses. If we were to throw out, put away, or rearrange some of the things that are cluttering the space, imagine what we could do. New space, new possibilities!

Let me give you an example of a new possibility. If I could just keep my piles of paper and mail organized, it would make both my husband and me happier. We would not have to look at clutter, and it avoids the conversation of who has the most mail in the pile. In addition, I would not have to waste time looking for things. Even when I have a good "sense" of where something is, I am wasting time looking for it. When I waste time, it either throws me off for something else I have to do, frustrates me because I cannot find it, or delays another, sometimes more pressing, need. Any of these things or situations prevents me from being in a space where I can see the Sacred, myself, or others clearly.

When I am moving through clutter, I am discombobulated and moving in circles, like the hamster spinning its wheel. If, however, I can move more freely and even expediently, I have room to generate new ideas, to plan the next steps, to figure out how to get around a problem, to have time for morning reflection and space with the Sacred, to take a little breathing time for myself, or to reach out to someone that I have been meaning to connect with for a year. Cleaning our sacred selves (mind, body, and soul) is no different. It opens the door for new beginnings, wonderful possibilities, and opportunities for us to help others as well.

Exciting Transformation—When we begin to move through the clean spaces of our lives, we have created a space for change to occur . . . to be transformed. We begin to see and view the Sacred, ourselves, and others differently. We might find ourselves seeing or hearing something we have seen and heard a thousand times but, suddenly, we gain new meaning and insight to it. It is analogous to cleaning a pair of eyeglasses. When we take our glasses off and use eyeglass cleaner—not the tail of our shirts, jackets, scarves, or dresses, but eyeglass cleaner—things look brand new. We can say, "Wow, I can see so much better." Until, however, we wiped them clean, we thought our vision was fine. Our transformation can only take place once we have done the necessary cleaning. We not only begin to see ourselves differently, but also the people around us. The following story illustrates this point.

A young, successful couple found their dream home. Shortly after purchasing it, the couple sat at their kitchen table to eat breakfast. The wife looked out the window and, to her surprise, she saw her neighbor hanging laundry on the clothesline.

"That laundry isn't clean. It's still dirty!" she said to her husband. "Someone needs to teach her a thing or two when it comes to washing her clothes!"

A couple of days later, the couple sat down at their kitchen table for a meal. The wife saw her neighbor hanging clothes on the clothesline. But this time, something was different.

"Wow, look!" the surprised wife said to her husband, "Her

clothes are clean! Someone must have taught her how to wash her clothes!" Without raising his head from his plate, the husband kindly responded, "Actually, honey, I got up early this morning and washed the window."*

And so it is with life—what we see when watching others depends on the purity of the window through which we look.[9] Washing our own windows from time to time changes our perspective.

Exercises and Reflection

Use the exercises below to help you begin to clean your house. Your perspective on life will change as your house becomes cleaner.

Close your eyes and allow your mind and body to settle down. Take a moment to take a deep breath to the count of five, hold your breath for five counts, and release for five counts. Repeat this several times. Once you have quieted your mind and removed all distractions, think about the rooms (areas) of your life that need cleaning. Try to focus on behaviors, thoughts, or circumstances that require deep cleaning.

Name the rooms or areas in your life that need to be cleaned in order for you to feel refreshed:

❧ What are the friendships or associations that need to be cleansed from your life in order for the Sacred to move more freely around and through you?

_____

_____

_____

❧ What are the thoughts, emotions, or patterns of behavior that you need to purge in order to "unclutter" yourself and make space for the Sacred?

_____

_____

_____

❦ What commitments are you willing to make to undertake the "cleaning projects" you listed above? Specify goals and deadlines whenever possible. Connect with someone who will hold you accountable to these commitments.

_____

_____

_____

CHAPTER 8

THE SIDE EFFECTS OF FEAR

Immediately he made the disciples get into the boat and go on ahead to the other side, while he dismissed the crowds. And after he had dismissed the crowds, he went up the mountain by himself to pray. When evening came, he was there alone, but by this time the boat, battered by the waves, was far from the land, for the wind was against them. And early in the morning, he came walking towards them on the lake. But when the disciples saw him walking on the lake, they were terrified, saying, 'It is a ghost!' And they cried out in fear. But immediately Jesus spoke to them and said,

'Take heart, it is I; do not be afraid.'

Peter answered him, 'Lord, if it is you, command me to come to you on the water.' He said, 'Come.' So Peter got out of the boat, started walking on the water and came towards Jesus. But when he noticed the strong wind, he became frightened and, beginning to sink, he cried out, 'Lord, save me!' Jesus immediately reached out his hand and caught him, saying to him, 'You of little faith, why did you doubt?' When they got into the boat, the wind ceased. And those in the boat worshipped him, saying, 'Truly you are the Son of God.'

–Matthew 14:22-33

Whether we believe such a miracle actually occurred, the lessons from the story are most relevant to how we handle fear in our lives. There is a little bit of fear in all of us and a great deal of fear in many of us. Some people are only afraid of certain things, like driving, flying, cats, dogs, certain kinds of people, etc. Some are afraid of trying new things, speaking in public, or taking a chance on love. Some people are simply afraid of change. Some fear their past will come back to haunt them; fear they will make a mistake in the present; and/or fear the future will not go well for them. Some fear walking down the street alone, walking in the park, or leaving their home. Some people fear and experience an overwhelming sense of worry and anxiety. Certainly, there are legitimate times for us to be afraid. Oftentimes, however, the side effects of our fears are more harmful than the thing that we fear.

The Side Effects of Fear

Fear can cloud our vision!—In the story at the beginning of the chapter, the disciples were so afraid that they could not recognize the obvious. They seemed to have reacted based on emotions; in this case, fear. Consequently, they were unable to see clearly, believing that Jesus was something that he was not . . . a ghost. It may, in fact, have looked that way to them. What is fear? False Evidence Appearing Real![10] False evidence that appears real is the same as cloudy vision. Cloudy vision prohibits us from hearing and seeing the changes we need to make:

❧ Cloudy vision prohibits us from hearing the voice of assurance, which is the voice of the Sacred gently urging us to move forward. It makes it difficult to hear that voice of familiarity that can soothe all of our doubts and fears. In fact, even when we hear the voice of the Sacred, we do not accept and trust what we hear and sometimes what we see. We can see miracles happening in front of us. We can see doors opening that were once closed. We can see opportunities springing up around us. Yet, we convince ourselves that the wonderful things that are happening are not meant for us. They are too good to be true or such things happen to other people and not to us.

❦ Cloudy vision prohibits us from making exciting, significant, and sometimes adventurous choices that may profoundly affect the rest of our lives. As an example, when we are young, sometimes fear keeps us from making choices about selecting colleges that are far away from home. Likewise, it keeps some parents from allowing their children to go away to college or to move out of their home . . . simply out of fear of what will happen when they leave. Despite our inability to see what will unfold in the future, we must rely on our relationship with the Sacred and with others to give us the assurance and faith we need.

Fear can impede our progress!—Like Peter, we can actually be moving forward. When we, however, suddenly look at the winds of chaos or confusion raging around us, we become paralyzed with fear, despite our progress. We get distracted by our surroundings and we panic. For instance, if we hear that our employer is downsizing, we may be moving along just fine until we see others around us becoming anxious. Panic begins to surface. Fear begins to immobilize us. The progress we were making grinds to a halt. Our fear prohibits us from growing or progressing further. Stunted progress prohibits us from moving in a positive direction.

❦ Stunted progress prohibits us from believing in the abilities of the Sacred, ourselves, and others. It creates a tendency to think about the negatives rather than the positives in a given situation. We must be careful not to become pessimistic, because our beliefs impact our actions, and our actions often can have grave impact on those around us. For instance, sometimes in life we are moving along with a promising future and something happens that causes fear to set in. We become afraid to take chances in life and begin to believe that something bad is always waiting around the next corner.

❦ When we carry pessimistic beliefs, we act in a way that opens the door to create more negative and fearful circumstances. In fact, we can perceive something as fearful, even when there is little evidence to support that fear. Our relationships with others are often impacted by our fears, and others may be limited in their choices based on our beliefs (e.g., if we had a negative experience with someone from a different racial or ethnic group, we might not allow our children to associate with that group). Consequently, we do not move forward nor do they move forward.

❦ Stunted progress prohibits us from taking the next step forward. For some of us, taking only a few steps is all we can manage or, rather, all we choose to manage. We move forward and become comfortable and complacent with our progress. We bask in the success of accomplishing our current goals but fear going beyond those goals. We say to ourselves, "Yes, I've stepped out on the water and taken a few steps, but I'm not going any farther. If I do, I might drown." While it is imperative that we learn to heed the inner voice of caution, it is equally important to heed the voice that beckons us to move forward on our journey.

Fear can be our downfall!—Fear not only stops us in our tracks, it can literally cause us to sink and drown. Think about what we are told to do if someone is trying to save us from drowning. We must try not to let panic or fear take control but, rather, move in the manner that they instruct us. If our fear takes over, it will cause us to believe that we are going to drown. When we fight, both of us can go under the water and drown. If we are faced with a fearful situation, we must calmly and assuredly keep on moving. We cannot stop in the middle of our progress. If we are a person who experiences a great deal of anxiety because of our fears, we can only make progress if we diligently and actively take steps to reduce those fears (even if we are still afraid). If, however, we become overwhelmed by our fears in the midst of trying and we stop working to overcome them, we run the risk of sinking into a dark place, believing that there is no hope for our situation. When fear becomes our downfall, we are further prohibited.

❧ We are prohibited from moving from a place of dysfunction, despite our desire for a different way of life. Think for a moment. We all know someone, have heard about someone, or have watched enough talk shows to be familiar with individuals who have experienced repeated sexual, physical, or emotional abuse. Initially they are afraid to trust anyone, especially in new relationships. Finally, they meet someone who treats them the way they need, want, and deserve to be treated. The relationship, however, does not last long. Something gets in the way. Often, that something is fear. Fear of the unknown leaves them unable to get used to the absence of dysfunctionality. And some of them end up in relationships—be it romantic or otherwise—that leave them in the same pit of despair they were in before. Likewise, people stay in other relationships that are destructive to the soul for fear of being alone. Fear can be our downfall, if we do not believe that we can move beyond our current circumstances. We must stand firm in our knowledge and faith that we are cared for by the Sacred and others who demonstrate their love for us.

Moving Toward Sacred Courage

Recall Previous Successes—When we are faced with fear, we have a tendency to be rooted in our present circumstances. We must recall the times that the Sacred has guided us through those challenging situations rather than going back to a place that promotes uncertainty and insecurity. If we can pause, take a deep breath, and think about past circumstances in which we faced fears and were able to prevail in the midst of those fears, we will garner strength to face our current situations. In the story above, if the disciples had simply recalled the miracle that had just taken place as well as the countless others they had witnessed, they would have suspected immediately that it was Jesus who walked on water.

Think Outside of the Box—When we allow fear to take control, we often revert to our old ways of thinking. When we move toward courage, we live in the knowledge that with the Sacred all things are possible. Even though we may never have seen anyone walking on water, we have witnessed or heard of some amazing things . . . things that we would have imagined impossible. Years ago, someone told the Wright brothers that it would be impossible for a plane to fly in the air. Thank goodness, their vision was not cloudy. They saw the impossible and kept striving toward their mark. Today, we all benefit from their clear vision.

Exercises and Reflection

Return to the story at the beginning of the chapter about Jesus and Peter walking on water. Close your eyes for a few moments and try to imagine yourself in Peter's place. Visualize yourself stepping out of the boat and onto the surface of the sea. Begin to walk as Peter did. Experience this as fully as you can by using your powers of imagination. When you have done so to your satisfaction, open your eyes, and journal responses to the following questions:

❦ What was it like for me to walk on water?

_____

_____

_____

❦ What did the wind and the waves seem to represent for me?

_____

_____

_____

❦ When in my life have I been given the chance to trust or the challenge to have faith but then faltered, due to my own fears?

_____

_____

_____

Now close your eyes again and reimagine the scene. This time, visualize calm waters and a soothing breeze. Imagine that you do not doubt; you do not falter; you do not sink. When you open your eyes, journal your response to this question:

❦ What is my new story of walking on water? (In other words: What would I do if I were free of fear?)

Part

III

SHARED RELATIONSHIPS

John's Story

Some years ago on a warm summer evening, as I sat in a restaurant with a colleague enjoying a sumptuous Italian meal, I heard a scratch on the window near where we were seated. Outside was a little boy, about eight years old, who was asking for food. Without delay, I signaled for him to join us, which he did, after I interceded with the maître d'.

"What would you like to order?" I inquired.

"A hamburger or hot dog with french fries," he responded.

"They don't serve that here. But how about some spaghetti and meat balls?" "Yes," he hesitatingly replied.

We talked for a while and I asked him his name and where he went to school. Where are your parents? Why are you out alone at this hour? Aren't you afraid of walking the streets at night? Without revealing too much, he said, "Mama's at work. I don't know my father. And my brother is in jail." As he struggled to use the knife and fork, we quickly realized that finger food was his daily fare. The idea of sitting around a family table was completely alien to him.

After dinner, I really felt guilty as the little fellow wandered off into the night on the same *Jericho Road* that had occasioned our chance meeting. I often wonder to myself whatever happened to him. Why didn't I follow up more? Was he able to survive a life of broken relationships—an uncaring father, an incarcerated brother, and a basic breakdown in family unity and coherence? For me, it was a missed opportunity to stretch the limits of love by going the extra mile. A lost opportunity to demonstrate that while he may not have known his paternal father, there was a heavenly Father who cared for him. Beyond a nice meal and movie fare, there were human agents here on earth who were instruments of God's love. Often, I use that experience as an example when discussing relationships, whether intimate or casual. God sets before us divine appointments each day. Our responsibility is to recognize and to act on them!

We are reminded that God wants us to be in relationship with our neighbor, and our neighbor is anyone in need of love, care, and compassion. God expects at least two things of us in our relationships with one another: (1) to be alert, and (2) to be available. To be alert is to be spiritually alert and aware of what is going on around us . . . to be perceptive of the human condition that is so often ignored in our daily routine and business.

Finally, God wants us to be available. Not just partially, but completely and sacrificially available to tend the wounds of a battered humanity. A humanity battered by loneliness, battered by neglect, battered by an inattentive society. God says, go the extra mile, even when it hurts . . . stretch the limits of your availability. There are many distressed souls scratching on the windows of our hearts, crying out for help.

Are we listening?

Carlton's Story

When I was a young boy, my father traveled often. As an administrator for a historically black college in Mississippi and later as an MBA student in Florida, he was in and out of the airport in Memphis—my brothers and I would ride with our mother to pick him up.

One evening, we went to get him and there was a young Middle Eastern man standing with my dad. He spoke virtually no English, and he was trying to meet up with his brother at Ole Miss about thirty miles from our home. That young man rode home with us. My father called his brother, who arrived about an hour later, tears of gratitude streaming down his face for the generosity and hospitality my father had shown.

The example my father set those many years ago continues to guide me to this day. In a greeting I sent to him for his sixtieth birthday, I reminded Dad of his encounter with the young Middle Eastern man. He seemed to have forgotten it altogether. Though it was not noteworthy to him, for me, he had been the living embodiment of higher consciousness—being willing to extend care and compassion to another simply on the basis of shared humanity.

Naturally, there were places we diverged. He would have preferred I married a woman and had children starting in my twenties. Instead, I remained unattached, and when I did partner for some years, it was with a man. Still, he always welcomed me home, and there was always a place for me in his heart.

In the late 1980s, my father became the first African-American mayor of my hometown. During campaign season, he received death threats that I didn't learn about until many years later. On election night, there was controversy as to whether his votes had been switched with those of his white opponent. In the midst of it all, Dad remained grounded and confident, never wavering in his commitment to serve *all* the people of the town. Eventually, the ballots were recounted, and he had clearly won. He was re-elected to two additional four-year terms, and to this day he is remembered for his inclusive approach to public service.

My father shared what he had generously, whether it was little or much, whether with family and old friends, or with people he was meeting for the first time. His and my mother's faith are the roots of my own abiding trust in the universe.

I wish for every child such fine examples of how to share with others. I am grateful for my dad and all that he taught me, just by being himself.

9

SHARED INTIMACIES

We Are All Interconnected

We have all heard the saying that no person is an island. We all live in relation to one another. What one person does impacts others. Despite the messages that promote "every person for him/herself" that we receive from jobs, commercials, television shows or otherwise, shared intimacies are necessary, unavoidable, and worthwhile.

Awareness of our connectedness can promote greater harmony and more positive outcomes within our relationships. We are able to understand that when we hurt others, we hurt ourselves. For instance, if a person is seeking a promotion in her job, she may spend more time at work than at home and may be unconcerned or unconscious about whom she hurts as she excels in her company. Her children might begin to resent her and act out at school, home, or some other forum. Ultimately, the children may grow disconnected from her, and she may be deeply hurt.

When we open our hearts to help another, it deepens our relationship with the Sacred and calls us to a place of goodness. And this goodness reminds us to live peacefully and in harmony with one another. We can accomplish more if we all work together.

Self-Reflection Is Important for Shared Intimacies

To learn to have healthier shared intimacies, we must first explore our own behaviors. We must examine ourselves to determine which of our behaviors contribute to disharmony. If we are having difficulty getting along with others, we must assess how we are communicating with them, by our words and by our actions. Do we typically look angry or stern when they approach us? Do we always have a negative comment? How do we invite harmony with that person or persons? We might have to ask ourselves if we are misinterpreting what the other person said to us. This may require us to stretch ourselves in ways that might be a little uncomfortable for us. We might have to use those smiling muscles more than the frowning muscles, even when the situations might incline us to do otherwise.

We cannot say everything we think, even if we think we are right. As we engage in self-reflection, it is important to examine how we communicate. We must listen first before speaking and be slow to become angry or defensive when others are speaking. Our words to others must be full of grace and seasoned with kindness. We have to look deep within our own souls and face what we do not want to face—our shortcomings.

We Must Value the Reasons for Change

Change must be accompanied by an understanding of why it is necessary to change. We must determine if the outcomes of our change have enough value for us to engage in the process. When we do not value change, we do not make the effort to change.

Our desires and reasons to change are often hindered by our thoughts that the other person is going to remain the same or that the other person is the one who needs to change. Perhaps there are qualities about ourselves that need changing in order for us to live a more fully evolved and enlightened life. To achieve change, we must raise our awareness to be more in line with the Sacred's desires for us. Our reason to change must come from a belief that a change in our behavior can elicit change in another individual. Keep in mind that small changes are better than no change.

Our inability to value the reasons we must change can be difficult when we have been hurt in some way. This hurt can cause us to be bitter not only toward those who have hurt us but to others around us, who do not have a clue about the emotional baggage that we carry. We find it difficult to value our reasons for change because we want to hold on to that pain and sometimes wallow in our self-righteousness. In order to value our reasons for change, we must meditate on the positive rather than focusing on those who have hurt us in some way. We must motivate ourselves to change by remembering to live harmoniously with one another and to deepen our relationship with the Sacred, enabling life-changing shared relationships with others.

Exercises to Promote Shared Intimacies

❦ Accentuate the positives.

❦ Think of a shared relationship in which you are experiencing disharmony.

❦ Take a moment to record on a sheet of paper or in a journal the positive aspects of that relationship.

❦ Record the positive qualities that you bring to the relationship.

❦ Record the positive qualities that the other person brings to the relationship.

❦ Spend time meditating on these qualities and determine if focusing on the positive rather than the negative will promote a healthier relationship.

Connections

❦ Think of a person you admire in one of your shared relationships. What qualities does she/he possess that you would like to have? What would it take for you to acquire these qualities?

❦ Make a list of the people in your life who you will use to support you as you seek to develop healthier shared intimacies (e.g., think of one person on whom you can rely to hold you accountable to your commitment to change).

Communicating with the Heart

❦ Practice a new way of communicating by giving others your full attention when engaged in conversation. Try to avoid distracting thoughts or considering the next point you want to make.

❦ Take a moment to reflect before responding immediately when the other person stops talking. Be sure to let them speak without interruption.

❦ Ask for clarification and repeat what you thought you heard the other person say, particularly in those circumstances where the conversations usually end in frustration. Express appreciation for others in your life.

❦ Listen for ways that you connect with others. Consider a point of view that differs from your own and try not to defend your position.

Reflection Questions

❦ What positive elements do you bring to your intimate relationships?

_____

_____

_____

❦ Do these elements generally work in your favor or do they, at times, create discomfort or frustration (e.g. if you are a giving person, do you seem to be the one always giving but rarely in the role of recipient).

_____

_____

_____

❦ What are some of your behavior patterns that enter into your shared intimacies that may contribute to disharmony?

_____

_____

_____

❦ What is the one thing that you would like others to know about you? How will their knowledge of this fact help to strengthen your relationships?

_____

_____

_____

❦ What would you like to change about or in your shared relationships?

_____

_____

_____

CHAPTER 10

ARE YOU THE BALM?

Is there no balm in Gilead? Is there no physician there? Why then has the health of my poor people not been restored?
—Jeremiah 8:22

There is a balm in Gilead to make the wounded whole. There is a balm in Gilead to heal the sin sick soul.
—African-American Spiritual

When I look around at all that troubles the world, I find myself asking "Is there no balm for the world?"

Is there no balm for this world, for the many who are suffering in some way, be it physically, emotionally, or spiritually? Is there no balm for the people of Darfur, Iraq, Afghanistan, or Syria to heal the souls of those who perpetuate violence and those who are victimized by it? Is there no balm for the Muslims who desire to practice their faith in unity and peace in this country, and for those who persecute them out of their own fear, ignorance, and grief? Is there no balm for the millions of women and children and men who are the victims of violence and sexual assault? Is there no balm for our teenagers who believe that sexting is a cool and popular thing to do? Is there no balm for people who want to break out in the entertainment industry but prefer to do so by sexually exploiting and exposing their bodies for millions to see?

Is there no balm for the children of Appalachia, other rural areas, and the inner cities where poverty is chronic? Is there no balm for the United States, whose education system has one of the largest educational disparities in the world between its white students and students of color? Is there no balm for those who have suffered terrible accidents, and for the family and community members who survive or are unharmed physically but must deal with the emotional scars? Is there no balm for those you pass on the streets who may be lonely, depressed, worried about financial problems, experiencing work or marital problems or peer pressure? Is there no balm for the one who has a life-threatening health challenge or the one who is in a spiritual slump?

The answer comes to me in the form of a question: "Are you the balm?" My answer: "Yes, I am the balm." What about you? Are you the balm? I believe that the Sacred is the ultimate balm. Yet, we are the manifestation of the balm. We are the balm incarnate! We are the balms available for healing, and it is time for us to apply the balm. I believe, however, that we do not apply the balm because we do not know its purpose, we do not know the instructions, and we do not know the potential for healing. I would like to share the lives of some people who have significantly impacted my life and who provided an example of how the balm might be applied. Each of them relied on their understanding of the Sacred and of spiritual teachings to help them lead a life of faith and servanthood.

Purpose of the Balm

First, I go to my mother, who is 90 years old, and my father, who was 86 when he died. My parents taught my nine siblings and me that we each had a purpose in life. My parents may not have known how the Sacred would ultimately use us or what our purposes in life might ultimately be, but they did know that we were to be in sacred relationships with one another. They instilled in us a compassion for others, a strong sense that it was important to help others whether it be through the words of a song, sitting and talking with someone, taking the needy some food, visiting the sick, or whatever we might do to lift others up. My parents knew the importance of demonstrating the Sacred's love in action.

As children, we did not always understand our parents' actions. We often wondered why they had to help those in need, even when others did not always show their appreciation. I recall a story from my childhood that illustrates my parents' application of their balm. A family moved in to the neighborhood who had very, very limited resources and limited education. The mental capacity of the parents was also limited.

My mother constantly gave the family whatever food supplies they came to borrow. One day, my nephew went to play with the two- to three-year-old grandchild of the family. I do not know what happened but the next thing we knew, the grandmother came to the door and asked to use our phone. We said, "Sure." She proceeded to call the sheriff to report that a little boy was playing with her grandson and had hit him. She wanted the sheriff to come and arrest him. She stood in OUR house, used OUR phone, and called the sheriff on OUR nephew. Unfortunately for her but fortunately for us, she was unable to tell the sheriff where she lived.

What do you think happened the next time she came to borrow something? My mother gave it to her. My mother understood that she was the manifestation of the balm. She could not hold on to a past slight or hurt. She was also aware that this woman's response was based on her limited problem-solving skills, and she knew no other way to handle the situation. My mother did not fault her for that but rather sought to live her life demonstrating love rather than disdain.

My parents ensured that we understood that we also were the balms. When the wife of an elderly couple had a stroke, my parents asked me if I would go stay with the couple for a while. I must tell you, I was in tenth grade, very much into my friends and myself, and I did not even care for the wife all that much. Taking care of her was the farthest thing from my mind. But when my mother asked me if I would go, my answer to her was yes. Truth be told, I did not think I had much of a choice because my parents raised us to be concerned for others. We were taught that in serving others, we served the Sacred.

I did not know it then, but I was the balm that was needed in that situation to help make the wounded whole. Later in life, while balancing children, family, and divinity school, I had to take care of my husband when he broke both of his legs. I learned that taking care of someone who is ill or disabled can be daunting. Who knows how my efforts served as a healing balm to this woman and her husband? Maybe, in some small way, my actions helped her husband handle some of his bigger decisions during that difficult time or even the smaller minute-to-minute tasks that come with caring for those who cannot care for themselves.

My purpose then and now is to be the balm that is needed to help heal others. What about you? Are you the balm for someone?

Application of the Balm

It's not enough for us to know our purpose as the balms. We have to know how to apply the balm. As with the aloe vera plant, it is one thing to know it can heal but quite another to know how to use it.

One of the greatest things about growing up in a small town is that everyone knew everyone else. When church events happened, you attended them whether it was the church of which you were a member or not. Often churches would work together to sponsor programs like Vacation Bible School (VBS).

One of the women who worked at VBS every summer was Mrs. Mattie Wilson. She passed away as a humble servant years ago, at the age of 101. She was a member of a neighboring church but was always my teacher for the weeklong VBS. What I remember the most about working with her is that she knew the directions for applying the Sacred's love—the balm that is needed for all of us. For without love, we grow up feeling insecure, lonely, angry, and dejected.

Mrs. Mattie applied the Sacred's love by showing us that she loved us as she loved herself. She developed a relationship with us, teaching us to demonstrate a love for ourselves in the way that we cared for ourselves, the way we spoke, the way we dressed and, yes, in the way that we responded to others. Mrs. Mattie understood that, even if we might find ourselves in a situation where the odds appear stacked against us, we are more than conquerors. We might feel persecuted or experience hardship or distress, but nothing can separate us from the love of the Sacred.

I believe that Mrs. Mattie knew how to apply the balm, for in connecting with us, she taught us to connect with the Sacred in us and the Sacred in others. And if we think about it, when we make this connection, we do not have any desire to hurt others or ourselves because we recognize that by doing so, we are hurting the Sacred.

The only way that Mrs. Mattie knew how to apply the balm was to be familiar with the sacred texts, which are the directions for how we are to live our lives and to help others along the way. We cannot apply the balm unless we read the directions (e.g., the Bible, Koran, Torah or whatever sacred texts are important to us). If more of us knew the directions, we would reach out more to those in need because, I believe, each of us is the balm that is needed to make the wounded whole.

Maybe you are the one to help end violence, persecution, suffering, hunger, conflict, or low school performance—whether it is in your neighborhood, your state, your country, or beyond. What directions do you need to help you apply the balm? I know that it can be overwhelming to think that you can help to heal the world. Know that, as the balm, you have unlimited healing potential, just as the aloe vera plant has great potential for healing certain types of ailments.

Potential for Healing

Mr. Mel, as we fondly called him, was the husband of the woman that I cared for after she had a stroke. Mr. Mel died nearly twenty years ago at the age of 104. I am sure that he never knew what a profound effect he had on me and so many others.

Mr. Mel had a fourth-grade education but was one of the smartest individuals I have known. He taught me much about the Sacred and opened my mind to deeper thought and understanding of sacred text, which for me was the Holy Bible. He always taught me the importance of seeking knowledge, not just what you learned in school but the knowledge of life. What is amazing about him is that he would say, "I have limited knowledge, but the knowledge is out there. You have to go and find it."

You see, he knew his healing potential and could point you to a different balm if he believed that his was not effective enough for the purpose at hand.

As important as it is to know your potential, it is equally important not to underestimate it. The reality is that the full potential of your balm may not be realized in your lifetime, but may be more like that of Mr. Mel's. A couple of years ago, I was asked to recall the people who had been significant to my spiritual growth and to write letters to those individuals. One of the first persons to pop into my mind was Mr. Mel. I realized that, in addition to my parents, he was one of the people who was not only open to my numerous questions about the Bible and attempted to answer them, but he also asked questions of me that forced me to consider the perspectives and life circumstances of others that might not fit neatly into my limited understanding of the Sacred.

You Are the Balm!

I believe that all of these people I have written about knew their purpose, knew their direction and their potential as balms. Their collective actions helped to reinforce the healing that each balm offered. I would not be the person I am today without their individual efforts.

Our efforts matter, whether or not we see the immediate results. Our application of the balm may be the very thing that keeps someone from going over the edge or inspires them to greatness! Our application of the balm also helps us to be the greatest that we can be. When we help others, we are able to find out more about who we are and our purpose.

I would like to offer a final thought that, just as we are to be the balm for others, it is crucial to understand that we often have to be our own balms. If there comes a time when we feel that we cannot make it or doubt that the Sacred has a purpose for us, consider Jeremiah 29:11, where we are told, "For surely I know the plans I have for you, says the Lord, plans for your welfare and not for harm, to give you a future with hope." We might also reflect on I Corinthians 2:9, where we read, "Eyes have not seen, nor ears heard, nor have entered into the heart of man the things which God has prepared for those who love him." There are other sacred resources that offer similar messages.

When you have trouble understanding how to apply the balm, consider that the Sacred is ever present with you. Virtually every spiritual tradition teaches us that we are in the Sacred and the Sacred is in us. If we rely on this awareness, we will be guided to those sacred teachings we need to call into remembrance at a given time, but we will also be guided in our daily decision-making.

When we doubt our effectiveness as a balm, remember that Moses was slow in speech and tongue. He thought that limited his potential to answer God's call. God said, "Who gives speech to mortals? Who makes them mute or deaf, seeing or blind? Is it not I, the Lord? Now go, and I will be with your mouth and teach you what you are to speak." (Exodus 4: 11-12). The great God who said "I am who I am." promises to be with us.

No matter who we are or what the situation is, the great "I am" is always with us. The Sacred has sent prophets and teachers into the world throughout the ages, and God is the ultimate balm. Yet, we must never forget that we are the manifestation. In this spirit, I ask you to consider that, "You are the balm."

Exercises and Reflections

❦ Look back over your past and think about a time when you were asked to perform a service you were not enthusiastic about performing. In your journal or the space below, record your thoughts about how that service may have been providing some much-needed balm in your own or another's life.

_____

_____

_____

❦ In your journal or the space below, write about some of the ways you have learned about effectively applying the balm, whether from those you have encountered in your life or by "reading the directions" in sacred texts such as the Bible or other inspirational writing.

_____

_____

_____

❦ Think for a moment about your own potential for healing others—
for being the balm. In your journal or the space below, rate your
potential on a scale from 0-10 (where 0 is the most self-centered
and callous person you know, 10 is the most loving, giving, and
healing person you know). Write about what factors influenced
your rating. Next, ask a few close friends and family members how
they would rate you and record their answers. How different were
their ratings from yours? What do you think accounts for those
differences? What would you need to do differently in order to be
able to rate yourself one digit higher?

_____

_____

_____

CHAPTER 11

STANDING IN THE GAP

David said to Abigail, 'Blessed be the Lord, the God
of Israel, who sent you to meet me today! Blessed be
your good sense, and blessed be you, who have kept
me today from blood-guilt and from avenging myself
by my own hand! For as surely as the Lord the God of
Israel lives, who has restrained me from hurting you,
unless you had hurried and come to meet me, truly
by morning there would not have been left to Nabal
as much as one male.' Then David received from her
hand what she had brought him; he said to her, 'Go up
to your house in peace; see, I have heeded your voice,
and I have granted your petition.'

—I Samuel 25:32-35

*O*n a brisk, cold, and snowy winter's day, I waited with
other passengers for the New York-bound train to arrive.
As I waited, my eyes were drawn to the big yellow sign
in black letters near the edge of the platform: WATCH THE GAP.
Truthfully, it seems that my eyes are always drawn to these
words each time I travel by train, as I am sure they are intended

to be. They are a reminder to me and all the other passengers to be careful when boarding the train. WATCH THE GAP because we might trip, fall, or hurt ourselves while getting on the train. WATCH THE GAP because our luggage wheels might get caught between the gap and the train. WATCH THE GAP because we might drop something between the gap, never to be recovered—at least not during this trip. WATCH THE GAP because there is potential for harm or danger.

These signs on the train reminded me of the gaps each of us has in our lives. Some of these are gaps that exist between us and the Sacred. Some of these gaps threaten to trip us up, to hurt us, or to knock us down, if we are not careful. They are the psychological gaps that can interfere with our relationship with the Sacred. Often, we need to be reminded to watch these gaps, for if we are watchful, perhaps we could avoid some of the potential negative attitudes, behaviors, and consequences that accompany these gaps.

These Are the Gaps of Our Lives

Disguised Gaps—Disguised gaps are the psychological gaps of inferiority that tell us we are not good enough to be a part of such a prestigious organization, to date that individual from such a prominent family, or to perform in the recital along with everyone else who seems so much better than us. They are psychological gaps of self-doubt that tell us that we do not deserve the promotion we got because "I really do not know what I'm doing." These types of gaps encourage us to give in to our fears, worries, or insecurities. They are psychological gaps of guilt that tell us as mothers that we do not need a break from our children who repeatedly call our names simply to get a rise out of us or to avoid thinking for themselves (e.g. "Mom, where did I put my shoes." "Mom, I don't see the milk." "Mom, mom, mom.").

Obvious Gaps—At other times, these gaps are more evident. They are gaps of despair that result from feelings of anxiety, depression, or loneliness. They are gaps of exhaustion and strain from taking care of a loved one who suffers from a physical, psychological, or mental illness. They are gaps of anger that well up inside of us from crying out to the Sacred to heal a loved one or to take her to glory rather than to let her suffer. They are gaps of financial hardship from bills that never seem to go away. They are gaps of stress from trying to balance ourselves on the tightrope of life.

Life in Between the Gaps

Strangely enough, remembering how others have stood in the gap reminds us that the Sacred has many avenues for providing the help that we need and for sustaining us during our weakest moments. These gaps, regardless of their size, can hinder us from experiencing the fullness of who the Sacred created us to be. They can also keep us from feeling the divine presence of the Sacred during our greatest times of need. So, it is imperative that we watch these gaps. But sometimes . . . sometimes we are not in a place where we can do our own watching.

We need someone to not just watch the gaps for us but to stand in the gap for us. It is especially during these times when the gaps between our current situation and the Sacred's love for us propel us into a crack and sometimes a gaping hole of confusion, frustration, or despair that we must remember those who have stood in the gap for us throughout the course of our lives.

In the story at the beginning of this chapter, David had been offended by the actions of Nabal, Abigail's husband, and wanted to take revenge. Abigail stood in the gap for David, who was at risk of going outside of the will of the Sacred. David was in danger of allowing the psychological gap of anger to lead him down a road of destruction, which ultimately would have impacted his relationship with the Sacred and perhaps even changed the course of history. This story describes David being so angry with Nabal for refusing to provide him with food after David had shown him kindness that he was going to kill Nabal and his whole clan. When Abigail learned of David's intentions, she sacrificed her own life to stand in the gap and save the lives of many. In our lives, we need an Abigail or perhaps multiple Abigails to stand in the gap when we are in jeopardy of losing ourselves, forgetting our purpose or wallowing in the gaps of our lives. Like David, we need Abigails who care enough to help keep us from blowing our tops and contributing to our own spiritual, psychological, and maybe even physical demise. Our Abigails must possess certain attributes, a few of which are below.

Courageous Abigail—Think about the role of women during this historic time. Abigail risked her life to go behind her husband's back to speak to David. If Nabal had found out, he would not have responded in a calm manner because, according to the story, he was an evil and foolish man. What if David had not responded to her so kindly? He was already filled with anger—ready to kill every man of Nabal's clan. She easily could have suffered that fate. In our lives, it is important to have an Abigail who will stand with us during difficult times, even if it means she (he) is risking something in her (his) own life, particularly if the outcome of the situation is for the greater good.

Trustworthy Abigail—We need Abigails who are trustworthy; people who are not simply trusted by us, but by others who surround us. For instance, we might be interested in hiring a friend or acquaintance, but we solicit the opinions of others to determine whether others have a positive view of the individual. When we are going to buy a car or look for a new hair salon or move to a different neighborhood, we might ask a trusted individual who specializes in a particular area to help us. Before committing to their help, however, we might ask others in our circle whether it's a good idea to seek the help of that individual. We rely on others to confirm our perception, to show us that they also trust the individual we are considering. Our Abigails need to be people that we can go to and share important yet difficult news. We must be able to rely on them to respond in a way that will benefit us. We must be assured that they will help us to make the right choices and that, when necessary, they will make the right choices on our behalves.

Strategic Abigail—Abigail had the servant quickly gather supplies for David and his army of men. She told him to go ahead of her, but she did not just rely on the servant taking the food to David. She understood the importance of being the one to sacrifice and to personally stand in the gap, rather than sending someone else to do the job. In this instance, the story indicates that Abigail knew that she acted as a servant of the Sacred. She knew that simply sending food would not satisfy David and might possibly fuel his anger more: too little, too late. She was strategic in her interception, considering various possibilities and consequences for the situation. Our Abigails must help us determine what steps will lead to the best outcomes and will help us move toward our long-term goals.

Wise Abigail—Abigail used the wisdom and intelligence given to her by the Sacred. She helped David to see that he would be taking matters into his own hands and not relying on the Sacred. Without her help, David would have been guilty of shedding the blood of innocent men. Without her help, David was jeopardizing his chances of becoming the King of Israel. Wise Abigails are able to assess the situation and determine how to address our current needs (e.g., reduce our anger) while simultaneously helping us to stay focused on the larger picture.

I know that Abigail's deferential behavior to David might be problematic to some: falling at his feet; cursing her husband; blaming herself for her husband's mistake; lavishing David with compliments and giving him good advice. Again, think of the time in which she lived. Think of the large gap she stood in . . . not just for herself but for Nabal's clan, for David and, ultimately, for the people of Israel. Abigail was wise enough to see that a moment of deference was more beneficial than years of suffering and grief.

Forward Thinking—Abigail was able to look at the long-term consequences. She understood that David was destined for something greater than the moment. His life could have been changed in the twinkling of an eye. David, who was considered to be a man after the Sacred's own heart, forgot in that moment that the Sacred desired more from him than to rule over a small number of men. The Sacred needed David to think beyond his current raging emotions and bruised ego. The Sacred needed David to think about the long-term plan: leading the Sacred's people. We need such Abigails to help us remember the Sacred's ever-present love, grace, mercy, and hopes for us.

On the Other Side of the Gap

Abigail stood in the gap and helped David to secure the Sacred's place for him in history. In doing so, Abigail also secured her place in history. Somewhere in Abigail's mind, she knew that it would be important for David to remember her down the line. Upon Nabal's death, David took Abigail as his wife and took over Nabal's clan, thereby gaining control over Hebron, where he was later king.

If Abigail had not been willing to stand in the gap for both Nabal and David, the result might have been her own demise. Even if she had survived David's violent reaction to Nabal, she might not have fared as well upon her husband's death. Abigail availed herself to be used by the Sacred and, in the process, she was able to assess her current situation, weigh the pros and cons and establish stability for herself in the future. When we are grounded in our relationship with the Sacred, serving as an Abigail helps to deepen our relationship with the Sacred and creates a stronger sense of who we are and the gifts we have been granted by the Sacred.

Are you willing to stand in the gap for someone who is not able to watch the gap in his or her own life?

Reflection

Many spiritual traditions speak of the virtue of sacrifice. Have you considered what sacrifices you are willing to make that will not only benefit you but also benefit others?

Examples of Standing in the Gap

What will you sacrifice in order to stand in the gap for someone else? Your time? Your energy? Your finances? Listed below are a few examples of standing in the gap.

- Tutor a child who is on the brink of failing a class or, worse yet, ready to give up on life because he does not have anyone taking an interest in his well-being.

- Drive an elderly person to an appointment, call her on the phone to say hello, or visit her home or nursing home to let her know that she is still valuable and important.

- Share your knowledge with others by volunteering in a school, a community organization, or a healthcare facility.

- Reach out to a troubled niece, nephew, or grandchild who does not seem to listen.

- Talk to the one who is distressed, taking the time to really talk to her about her hopes, fears, and dreams, even if you are pressed for time.

12

BE CAREFUL WHAT YOU THINK

Finally, beloved, whatever is true, whatever is honourable, whatever is just, whatever is pure, whatever is pleasing, whatever is commendable, if there is any excellence and if there is anything worthy of praise, think about these things. Keep on doing the things that you have learned and received and heard and seen in me, and the God of peace will be with you

—**Philippians 4:8**

What we think in life determines our outlook and our outcome. For instance, if our thoughts are positive and uplifting, we may be more likely to give others the benefit of the doubt when they have behaved in an offensive manner. On the other hand, if our thoughts are negative and judgmental, we are likely to become angry and hostile toward others when their actions are offensive. Unfortunately, some of us are wired to think negatively most of the time. However, we do not recognize this pattern of thinking. We do not understand that our negative thought patterns, which are really limited thought patterns, keep us from seeing the beauty in the world and in the people around us.

Again, what we think matters and has consequences for our lives. Think for a moment about the following saying: Sow a thought; you reap an act. Sow an act; you reap a habit. If you sow a habit; you reap a character. If you sow a character; you reap a destiny.[11]

Therefore, it is crucial that we work on our thought patterns. How do we do that when thinking negative is such an easy thing to do? How do we avoid conforming to this negative thought pattern and renew our minds in order to think about what is good and loving? The following techniques are useful in transforming our thinking. They are not hierarchical but necessary to changing thought patterns.

Be Mindful

Often we gripe and complain so much that we do not even recognize when we do it. It is second nature for us. In order for us to be conscious of what we are saying, doing, and thinking, we have to practice mindfulness. Simply put, mindfulness is an act of being in the moment, not in the moment ahead or the moments behind us. It means being aware of what we are thinking in the moment. If we deliberately pay attention to what comes to our minds and out of our mouths, we become more conscious and mindful of what we are saying, and then we learn to change our thought patterns. Louise Hay, in her book *You Can Heal Your Life*, states, "It is only a thought, and a thought can be changed. I am not limited by any past thinking. I choose my thoughts with care.

I constantly have new insights and new ways of looking at my world. I am willing to change and grow."

Be Attentive

Once we are mindful of what we are thinking and committed to changing our thought patterns, we can then practice being attentive—attentive to what needs to be said. All too often, when we engage in conversations with others, we already know how we are going to respond before they have finished their sentences. This type of practice indicates that we are not attentive to the other individual nor are we attentive to the Sacred's voice, which might prompt us to respond differently than we intended. It is important to pause for a number of seconds between sentences in order to hear what needs to be said rather than the unnecessary verbiage that comes when we are not attentive to the Sacred's voice.

Think Again

Frequently, we misinterpret situations. We think someone intentionally set out to harm us in some way or we believe them to be inconsiderate, failing to think of anyone but themselves. We fail to give them the benefit of the doubt. We think the worst. We have all been there. Think about the times that we have blamed someone for losing our keys, forgetting that in our haste we put them in a different spot than usual; blamed someone for using the last of the detergent or all the gas in the car, then remembering we were the last one to do laundry or drive the car; or accused someone of not responding to our emails or invitations, and then realizing we never sent it. Further, think about when someone says something that offends us. We make all sorts of judgments about their behavior and who they are as a person, without considering why they might have made such statements. We must consider all the possibilities, rather than rely on our usual thought patterns: They are out to get me or do not care about me or are just plain inconsiderate. The list goes on.

Remove Ourselves

An important step in evaluating the evidence or considering all the possibilities is to remove ourselves from the equation. Recognize that the person's responses to us or their patterns of behavior are not about us. More likely, their responses and behaviors are about them and their idiosyncrasies, anxieties, needs, etc. Their lifelong experiences have shaped their patterns of behavior, and they are simply responding to us based on these patterns and their interpretation of our behaviors based on their past experiences. When we are able to recognize that it is not about us, our response patterns are different.

Reframe It

I was speaking one day to a woman (whom I will call Nancy), and she was complaining about her mother, who had a tendency to interfere with situations that did not concern her. On this occasion, Nancy's mother had called to dictate when Nancy's husband should arrive at her parents' home to help her father complete a project. In fact, she thought he should already be there and was emphatically explaining this fact to Nancy over the phone while Nancy's husband was in the background demanding that her mother "mind her own business."

Nancy was clearly frustrated to be caught in the middle but more frustrated at her mother's interference, particularly because a set time had been predetermined by her husband and father to meet and complete the project. To help Nancy reduce her frustration around her mother's behavior, I helped her to reframe her thinking about the situation. Aware that her mother was going through chemotherapy treatment for cancer and had days of complete physical and emotional exhaustion, I suggested she look at this situation as, "At least my mother is feeling better. She is having a good day physically and back to her old self." Nancy laughed and acknowledged that, surprisingly, reframing her thinking made her feel much better. We can learn to save ourselves so much headache and worry if we learn to put a positive spin on a situation.

Look Beyond

Often when we are in the midst of anger, frustration, or despair, we find it difficult to see a bright side. Though it may be difficult, we must begin to unpeel the layers that prevent us from seeing the core of the situation. Such is the case when we have experienced physical or emotional hardship. Our shell and protective coverings may harden over time but, if we try hard enough, we will uncover that something good lies underneath the surface. It is that goodness that we must focus on because it will open an avenue to uncover future goodness and brighter tomorrows.

Remove Negativity

Harmful Relationships—There are some people who are just plain toxic. Every time we talk to them they have something bad to say. We give them good news and they will find a way to turn it into something negative.

"Guess what? I got a new job today. It's in the city."

"In the city, are you sure you want a job in the city? Such a hassle going back and forth."

Sometimes these people are so toxic that the energy of the room changes when they enter, and we did not even realize how tense we were until they left. These are the people we need to remove from our lives. If we choose not to remove them from our lives, we must learn to express our disapproval of their behaviors and our unwillingness to listen or take part in their actions. For instance, if we find ourselves in a situation where a person or a group of people are speaking negatively about someone else and we are not in agreement with their comments and behaviors, we must voice our concerns or remove ourselves from the conversation.

Hazardous Waste—People are not the only source of toxicity. Media is equally toxic and can, at times, be a hazardous waste. Individuals who already have negative, depressed and/or paranoid thinking, will not benefit at all from programs that investigate the behavior, personality, and minds of criminals. In fact, such shows can be detrimental to our well-being. Movies, television shows, music, magazines, and social media that perpetuate violence, sexism, classism, racism, etc., subtly paint a picture of negative and potentially hazardous behaviors. We have to remove these harmful images and thought patterns from our lives.

Dig Deeper

In my experience with teenagers, they often complain that their parents only notice the negative things they do and not the positive. While talking with a teenage girl and her mother during a session, the teenager remarked through tears that even when she works hard to help clean the house, her mother, upon returning home, only notices what she did not do. Likewise, when teenagers have exhibited behaviors that are troublesome, their parents might not notice when they have modified those behaviors in some way. The same is true in marital relationships, partner relationships, or work relationships. We might make statements like "you always" or "you never." Often, the results are poor self-worth, continuous frustrations, contentious relationships, and overall lack of desire to try and modify behavior.

As a therapist, I often ask clients to look for the small changes in themselves or others and acknowledge that they recognize these changes. When they acknowledge such changes and look for whatever is true, noble, right, pure, excellent, and praiseworthy, they will begin to feel better about themselves and desire to make even more changes.

These techniques might be hard, especially in the beginning. It will take some practice to be mindful, evaluate the situation, reframe the thinking, remove negativity, and go beyond the surface to look for positivity. To help themselves move forward, these individuals must look for positive people to imitate and for strong encouraging examples to help us. If these things are done, here is the wonderful assurance: The Sacred's peace will surround them.

Recall the scripture at the beginning of the chapter! "Finally, beloved, whatever is true, whatever is honorable, whatever is just, whatever is pure, whatever is pleasing, whatever is commendable, if there is any excellence and if there is anything worthy of praise, think about these things." In other words, meditate on these things.

We cannot have the fullness of the Sacred's anointing in our lives if we spend a lot of time rolling around in our minds all the things that are wrong with our circumstances and with the rest of the world. How are we going to have happy marriages when we keep gathering evidence about how our spouses cannot ever get anything right? How are we going to enjoy our children when we cannot let go of mistakes they made in the past? How are we going to find a job when we are so critical of ourselves that it leaves us paralyzed and unable to recognize our own gifts?

MAXIMIZE YOUR SACRED INTELLIGENCE

*N*ow in Jerusalem by the Sheep Gate there is a pool, called in Hebrew Beth-zatha, which has five porticoes. In these lay many invalids—blind, lame, and paralysed. One man was there who had been ill for thirty-eight years. When Jesus saw him lying there and knew that he had been there a long time, he said to him, 'Do you want to be made well?' The sick man answered him, 'Sir, I have no one to put me into the pool when the water is stirred up; and while I am making my way, someone else steps down ahead of me.' Jesus said to him, 'Stand up, take your mat and walk.' At once the man was made well, and he took up his mat and began to walk. Now that day was a sabbath. So the Jews said to the man who had been cured, 'It is the sabbath; it is not lawful for you to carry your mat.' But he answered them, 'The man who made me well said to me, "Take up your mat and walk."' They asked him, 'Who is the man who said to you, "Take it up and walk"?' Now the man who had been healed did not know who it was, for Jesus had disappeared in the crowd that was there. Later, Jesus found him in the temple and said to him, 'See, you have been made well! Do not sin anymore, so that nothing worse happens to you.'

–John 5:2-14

Our relationships with the Sacred, ourselves, and others are defined by the choices we make and our desire to begin and continue our journeys toward healing. In order for any of these relationships to flourish, we must take a hard look at ourselves and ask ourselves the tough questions that will help us move forward.

We must examine the steps we have taken and determine whether we are actually moving along our journeys to healthier relationships or are we stuck at a particular point along the path. Sometimes, it can feel as though we are doing the right thing when, in fact, we are simply going through the motions—walking the right paths but getting nowhere. In this final chapter, we must reflect on the work we have done to create healthier relationships and to heal broken relationships. We must explore whether we have fully tapped into our Sacred source to inform our decision-making or approached our healing in a hesitant, self-sabotaging or static manner. In other words, are we really using our *Sacred Intelligence* or are we going through the motions. Four questions help to guide our thinking as we continue to strive toward our goals.

Do You Want Healthier Relationships?

The man in this passage had been sick for thirty-eight years and was waiting by the pool, next to the smelly sheep, waiting to be healed when Jesus came along. When Jesus saw him, he asked "Do you want to be made well?" Why would Jesus ask such a seemingly ludicrous, silly, and simple question?

Was this man not sitting there like all the other invalids waiting to be healed? I think Jesus asked because this invalid was like many of us. We walk around with afflictions, some of us for thirty-eight years like this man—afflictions that paralyze us in some way.

For instance, we have made or heard someone else make such paralyzing statements. "I'm just not good in math." "I'm bad with money." "I'm not talented." "I can't exercise because I've got problems with my health. I have some other medical conditions that prohibit me." "I've done some things that are unforgivable and I'm ashamed." "I can't leave this relationship. How would I survive?" "I'm an alcoholic. My father was an alcoholic. My grandmother was an alcoholic. That's what I am."

The excuses go on and on. We are afflicted with emotional problems, physical ailments, spiritual despair, and social ills. We cry out to the Sacred, begging for healing. We claim we want to be better. Often, however, we are just sitting around the pool with the other invalids.

I believe inherent in the question "Do you want to be made well?" is an understanding that our healing begins with *our* desire to be healed. But how badly do we want to be healed? Do we really want what we say we want? We look the part. We act like it. We come to the pool often (e.g., taking time out with the Sacred, examining parts of ourselves, trying to be understanding of others). Are we coming to the pool to take full advantage of our healing opportunities? Are we simply jumping on the latest bandwagon because it's what everyone else is doing? We do not really believe our relationships will get better.

Yes, there are times in our lives that we go through the motions (recall the mirror exercises presented in Chapter 2) because it is a step in the right direction. But at some point, our belief has to kick in. And when it comes to our healing and changing our situation, the question is: Do we really want what we say we want? Do we desire it?!

Also inherent in the question "Do you want to be made well?" is the idea that some of us have become so accustomed to our afflictions, circumstances, and relationships that we really do not want to change. We choose to remain in the situation that we know rather than venture into the unknown. We are guided by the pessimistic rather than the optimistic *"What if."* Sometimes, unknowingly, we are comfortable with our stories, even if they are chaotic, depressing, and burdensome. We do not want to rewrite them or do the necessary (often daunting) work to change them. Like the man at the pool, we are waiting for the "troubling of the waters" but are not really ready to change in order to have healthier relationships. What about you? Do you really want what you say you want? Healthier relationships?

What Are Your Excuses?

The man responded to Jesus' question by saying that when the water is troubled, he has no one to help him into the pool and someone else always gets there before him. His response sounds good and reasonable. Yet, it also sounds like an excuse, similar to our own excuses.

What are we doing when we "get" to the many pools of healing that are opportunities to change our lives? Are we standing around waiting on someone else to help us take the final plunge?

"Someone else got there first and they got the job." "No one will cut me a break." "I don't know the latest technology." "I can't speak the way they do." "I can't work as fast as they can." "I can't start over." "I'm not as smart." "I can't get to this medical office." "I can't afford to start my own business." "I can't get past the loss, the hurt, the pain, the abuse." "I can't. I can't. I can't!"

We have to want our circumstances to change badly enough to do whatever it takes—to go the extra mile. Change might require moving some other people out of the way. Change might require us asking someone else to assist us. Change might even require us going through a painful process, be it psychological, emotional, or physical, if that is the necessary prescribed treatment in order for us to reach our healing (e.g., pain of feeling lonely or struggling financially in order to leave a destructive relationship; pain of withdrawal symptoms in order to be freed of an addiction, etc.). Change might require us going against the grain and thinking outside the box, as discussed in previous chapters.

We must ask ourselves and tap into our sacred source to determine whether there is only one way to be healed. If we look a bit more closely at this passage, we can see that our healing is often right in front of us but is limited by the steps we take. Reflect for a moment on this story. At a certain time, the water was stirred. Those who were able to get in were healed. Those who could not get in were not healed. So even though the water was so close, healing could not happen without fully immersing oneself in the water. There was no half-stepping or getting healed by proxy. So, the implication is that we must invest in the full opportunity because investing partially is not good enough to accomplish our goal. If we are too busy looking at what we cannot do, we will never be healed of our afflictions.

Sometimes, we can be in such despair that our healing has not occurred that we cannot even think beyond the present. Sometimes, we are so busy looking at our current realities that we cannot imagine that life could be different. We simply cannot visualize it. Even in our despair or our current realities, we must keep coming to the pool. We must come to the pool to keep practicing and believing in our healing and the possibility of change.

If we practice and believe, we begin to behave as if what we are seeking already exists. Moreover, we began to visualize and gain clarity regarding the number of ways that our goals might be accomplished. So, we must not make excuses. We have to go all the way and act as if we have already manifested what we are pursuing. Because one day, something is going to happen so magnificent that we are going to be healed of our circumstances and the avenue will be opened for us to have healthier sacred, selfish, and shared relationships . . . maybe not in the way we expected or practiced for but even more spectacularly.

In the passage from the Gospel of John, the man immediately rose and walked at the command of Jesus. He experienced immediate healing. He did not have to get in the pool or go through the customary steps. Like this man's experience, doors and opportunities for change are opened by the Sacred or others in our path. Doors we never expected to open. We simply have to desire a new way of being for us (even if that new way of being is to change our attitude about our circumstances) and not make excuses when the time comes. For instance, this invalid man did not say, "I cannot carry my bed on the Sabbath." He certainly could have made that excuse but chose to take advantage of the situation. We must ask ourselves if we are taking advantage of our opportunities for healing or are we making excuses?

Do You Express Gratitude To The Sacred And Others For Changes In Your Life?

Interestingly enough, this man did not seem to have any awareness that the one who healed him claimed to be the Son of God. It does not appear that he stopped to think about how it was possible that he could be healed by a simple command. He merely focused on his healing and was grateful. He did what was customary and went to the temple. Although he might have gone because it was required to be examined by the priest, I would like to believe that he went to acknowledge the awesomeness of the Sacred and to offer praise for his healing. He did not become so overjoyed at his ability to walk after thirty-eight years that he began to rush around and exclaim the good news to everyone. Instead, he went immediately to the temple.

Sometimes, we get so excited about the new things taking

place in our lives that we forget to thank and praise the giver. It is precisely during these times that we must stop and acknowledge the presence and role of the Sacred in our lives, guiding and ever directing our journeys. Such an acknowledgment allows us to express gratitude and prompts us to spend intimate time with the Sacred in order to reap the many wonderful benefits of this relationship.

We must remember to fit our hectic schedules around the time we have set aside for the Sacred and not the other way around. If we make time with the Sacred essential, our *Sacred Intelligence* becomes almost second nature, and we will learn to be grateful for the daily gifts we receive (miraculous or otherwise). We began to appreciate the Sacred's prompting, our own efforts, and the valuable support we receive from others. We will recognize that, although we may feel alone or in control of our own lives, we are still utterly dependent on the relationships that we have with the Sacred and with others. For that, we must be forever grateful.

Finally, Do You Want To Maximize Your *Sacred Intelligence*?

We can have amazing healthy relationships! Such relationships, however, only come after we have done what is necessary to heal our inner beings, which begins with recognizing the unconditional love and abiding presence of the Sacred. This recognition opens the door for greater insights into the psychological, physical, emotional, and spiritual pain that shapes our views of the world and greatly impacts our selfish and shared relationships. These insights are powerful but useless if we do not make the necessary changes to heal our inner beings. We have everything we need for our healing. The question is "Do you want to be made well?" I believe that you do and know that you can.

If you have worked through the exercises in this book, you are one step closer in your journey to healing. Accessing and using *Sacred Intelligence* requires daily practice and a firm commitment. The more you use it, the better you become at making choices that will honor the Sacred, manifest your greatness, and recognize the sacred and humanity of others.

I wish you profound love, happiness, and peace as you learn to maximize your Sacred Intelligence and travel on your sacred, selfish, and shared journeys toward healthier relationships.

NOTES

1. While the "Sacred" is used throughout this book to refer to a divine presence, "God" is used in certain contexts because it is the frame of reference for the individuals in some of the stories.

2. Scriptures are taken from the New Revised Standard Version: Harpers Collins Publishers (2007).

3. See note 1.

4. *Rock of Ages* is a hymn written in 1776 by Augustus M. Toplady.

5. The words from this song are taken from *His Eye Is on the Sparrow,* originally written in 1905 by Civilla D. Martin.

6. Wolpe, David (1993). *Teaching Your Children About God: A Modern Jewish Approach.* Henry Holt and Company, Inc.: New York, NY.

7. Battle, Michael (1997). *Reconciliation: The Ubuntu Theology of Desmond Tutu.* Pilgrim Press: Cleveland, Ohio.

8. Brach, Tara (2004). *Radical Acceptance: Embracing Your Life With The Heart of a Buddha.* Bantam Dell: New York, NY.

9. The author of this illustration is unknown. Some version of this illustration is widely used and circulated by many faith traditions, including Christian, Islam, and Judaism, as well as other individuals and groups seeking to inspire us to examine our own lives before judging others. It is found on multiple websites.

10. The origin of this widely used acronym is unknown, but it is believed to have been around since the 1950s.

11. *Sow a thought; you reap an act. Sow an act; you reap a habit. If you sow a habit; you reap a character. If you sow a character; you reap a destiny.* This quote has been attributed to Charles Reade, Samuel Smiles, and Ralph Waldo Emerson.

ABOUT THE AUTHOR

Terrlyn L. Curry Avery, PhD, MDiv, is the founder of Sacred Intelligence, LLC, a counseling practice where she merges spirituality and psychology in her treatment of individuals with psychological and emotional problems. As a licensed psychologist and ordained minister in the Presbyterian denomination, she is rigorous in not imposing her religious and spiritual beliefs upon her clients. Rather, she and her staff guide individuals, couples, families, and groups as they recognize their divine power to make intelligent choices that will transform their lives—mind, body, and soul. She is the host of the public access TV program *Sacred Intelligence With Your Host Dr. Terrlyn L. Curry Avery*. Dr. Curry Avery has a PhD in Clinical and School Psychology from Hofstra University, a master of divinity degree from Yale University, a master of arts in psychology from American University, and a bachelor of science in psychology from Howard University. Dr. Curry Avery lives in Connecticut with her husband, two children, and rambunctious dog.

Sacred Intelligence
The Essence of Sacred,
Selfish, and Shared Relationships

Terrlyn L. Curry Avery

www.sacredintelligence.com

Publisher: SDP Publishing

Also available in ebook format

TO PURCHASE:

Amazon.com

BarnesAndNoble.com

SDPPublishing.com

www.SDPPublishing.com

Contact us at: info@SDPPublishing.com

CPSIA information can be obtained
at www.ICGtesting.com
Printed in the USA
FFOW05n2352120215

9 780990 559672